i've had one too
a story of abortion and healing

Anna Wood

Published with Numinous Books.
Cover art by Louiseandrolia.com
Interior layout by Chriswilliamsdesign.co.uk
ISBN: 978-1-7354710-4-4
www.the-numinous.com

for my family

introduction

How can any of this possibly matter?
I am sitting in yet another meeting at work. All of the conference rooms in our office building are named after dinosaurs from Jurassic Park and the one I'm in is called *Velociraptor*. I'm here with the company stakeholders and we're reviewing our roadmap and backlog. Corporate strategy. Product direction. All I can do is gaze out the window towards the mountains in the distance. The glare in this room is always intense, and the strength of the Arizona sun whitewashes the horizon. The sterility and dampened sound of the conference room make the world outside seem more like a screen and less like reality.

My CEO asks me a question. I have no idea what he just said, and I am forced to ask him to repeat himself. "Are we still on track to begin Alpha testing the new dashboards by Q1 of next year?" I mumble a response and focus on the numbness in my mouth—the result of a dentist appointment earlier that day.

I'm lost in my own world. Five days ago, I was pregnant. A life full of opportunity lay ahead of me. I shattered that vision with an abortion. Now I feel lifeless. As if by ending the life inside me, the whole world should have ended with it. And yet here I am, a host of contradictions. I am numb, and I feel everything as keenly as if cacti were scraping my bare skin. When I'm not in meetings I am a train wreck, running down to the parking garage multiple times per day to cry and then try to pull myself back together. Each day is an interminable series of seconds and minutes and hours. Life has whittled it-self down to segments of time, each of which has to be endured until I can fall into a few hours of dreamless sleep where I do not know what I've done and who I feel like I've become. Although sleep is a respite, I wake up in the mornings to find the clock still ticking.

In meetings like this one, where my focus is lost, where I've lost even myself, all I can do is wonder: *how can any of this possibly matter?*

AT THE TIME OF WRITING this introduction, it has been 14 months since I had the abortion, and I look back at that decision and I wonder: could I have made it work? Could I have created a happy life both for myself and for that child? Most days my answer to that question is "yes." I have made sweeping changes in my life since then. I've gone from feeling stuck and unable to move forward in my life to feeling free and excited about new possibilities. I moved on from a relation-ship I felt trapped in, moved away from a city that wasn't working for me, and, most importantly, I have learned that it's the hardest of times that bring about the most significant changes. Life is a Ferris wheel. At the bottom I lost my sense of self, and the ability to trust my intui-tion; there were so many dark emotions, and so much confusion and stagnation. On my way up I found out what I was made of, and now, at the top, I am experiencing the joy of a life built on integrity. I do what I know to be right and have clarity on what that is.

I couldn't see any of this when I decided to have my abortion. All I could see was a black hole of fear and pain and guilt that I thought would last forever. I was in a relationship that made me feel isolat-ed and lonely. When we spoke, we fought. When we tried to work through our issues, he negotiated our differences like the broker he was, while I could do nothing but cry. I woke up each morning in his bed choked with anxiety. Faced away from him, curled up against the edge of the mattress, each part of my body felt like it was on fire.

But he was all I had. Besides him, there were few people I felt I could talk to about being pregnant. As far as I knew, my friend Laura was the only woman in my circle who'd had an unplanned pregnancy or an abortion. It had happened 15 years ago, and it was a decision she had always had great peace with. I leaned on her heavily for support and she was unwavering. I was terrified to tell anyone else, afraid of being judged because of the circumstances of the pregnancy and the fact I was even considering having an abortion. I can see now that this was mostly a reflection of how harshly I was judging myself.

If I'd only known how many of my friends had one too—friends whose children call me "auntie," who had seen me through the worst of my depression, whom I've sat with through parents' deaths and career upheavals—maybe things would have gone differently for me. Perhaps after hearing how hard an abortion was for some of those women, I would have continued down the path of parenthood with my then boyfriend. Maybe I still would have had the abortion, but not hated myself quite so much, not labeled myself a monster.

I can't say for sure if anything would have gone differently had I had a couple of other friends to reach out to, but I imagine connecting with more people about this would have eased the isolation, made me feel more secure in my decision, and, perhaps, may have changed my internal narrative about the kind of person my decision revealed me to be.

I'm writing this book with the hope that it reaches a woman in need, and that I can be that extra friend for her, the friend I wish I'd had. Maybe this book will help open up a conversation about this most taboo of topics, and help any woman feel less like *she's the only one*. Stories have the power to heal, whether you're the one telling them or hearing them. I sought out the stories of abortion among the women in my life to help myself through this time. It's tough. Sometimes these stories are told only to our most trusted companions, more often we tell them only to ourselves, tucked away in a journal or a hidden corner of our soul. It has been no surprise to see how few personal narratives of abortion are in the public domain today. It begs the question: how do we get women to talk about this openly?

In the 1960s, empowered by the Women's Rights Movement, and with abortion seen as a key issue in terms of gender equality, women spoke publicly and frequently about their abortions. As the movement waned through the 1970s, 80s, and 90s, women once again became fearful of talking about their abortions. In her 2019 book *Without Apology*, Jenny Brown explains that "it was the strength of the movement—the organized power of sisterhood—that made speaking out possible for so many." She goes on to explain that today, "we must organize to stick together and support each other, to blunt the attacks and isolation that may result from telling the truth." Her words resonate so strongly with me. On the one hand, I want to be open about the choice I made to help women feel less "other" for making the same choice themselves. But still, I hesitate to do so publicly because of the hate and judgment I know I will face from others. I hope this book, and other stories like it, pave a way for us all to be more open about our abortions to further break down deeply rooted stigma surrounding this issue.

IN THE WEEKS AND MONTHS that followed my fateful visit to the clinic—the one where I swallowed the handful of pills that would forever alter my life path—I was raw and nervy. My thoughts were a hot stone that I couldn't hold in my hand. Over time, I was able to see things with a softer mindset and stay with my feelings a little longer. Through mindfulness meditation and work with a life coach, I began to recognize that I could survive each passing thought and emotion as I felt it. With time and practice, the ups and downs lost some of their power over me. I was able to forgive myself here and there, and eventually I began to even question whether or not I needed to be forgiven in the first place. This new vantage point is what finally allowed me to open up to my friends, albeit haltingly. What greeted me on the other side was the opposite of what I'd anticipated. Where I had expected my friends to distance themselves from me, or even to be disgusted by me, instead I found warmth and love, honesty and compassion, and a library of untold stories about the reproductive lives of the women I love. Their openness and strength were a warm embrace after having been alone in the cold for so long.

Once, during this period of liminal space, I was stuck in traffic on the 101 in some cloudy weather. At the time I was commuting one week per month between Arizona and California for work, having recently moved to the coast. On this particular trip I'd rented a minivan so that I could move my houseplants. I had a plan to move to California for good, and the inside of the rental looked like a jungle, the plants swaying precariously any time I took a turn too sharply. Now, the traffic at a standstill, I popped my headphones in and took the opportunity to call my friend Abby and catch up about our lives.

Abby and I had been co-workers, but she had recently moved on to another company, so our opportunities to connect had become less frequent. During the course of our conversation, I had to catch myself several times when I nearly mentioned the abortion. This woman knew *everything* about me—except this. It felt like a stain on me and the integrity of our relationship. I wore my unspoken truths like a fake smile that never quite made it to my eyes. Sitting in the van, a paraglider was circling overhead, drifting back and forth over a tall, grassy dune next to the beach. He finally made a fast but safe touchdown. I had to tell her.

She was surprised, certainly, but treated me gently and with love. Something I had been struggling to do for myself. We carried on chatting, and after quite some time she said something about *after my own abortion*. Wait, what? Back it up. I had no idea. She told me she was certain she had mentioned this before and was surprised that I didn't know. I *did* know she was on the board of Planned Parenthood, so it made some sense. But she was also Catholic and a mother of two—one of the most loving and caring women I knew. The kind of strong woman who survived her son's childhood bout with cancer, and who had used that experience to counsel others with love and compassion. Back then, I struggled to marry these attributes with a woman who'd had an abortion. Weren't *women like us* supposed to be selfish, soulless baby killers?

There was more to her reproductive history too, which came out in the following months over many dinner dates, where our conversations were interrupted by laughter and tears. We favored local cafes with close seating, and among the clanking of dishes and low chatter of nearby tables, I can vividly remember swinging from whispers to loud peals of giggles that turned all the heads in the restaurant to us. I remember Abby's warm hugs at the end of our meals and how much her support and love buoyed my spirits. I wished we'd had these conversations—I wish I had heard *her story*—a long time ago.

I remembered those conversations that day on the freeway. Finally, the traffic began to move, and I made my way back home. I sat in my newly leafy living room and found myself wondering: how many other women in my life have gone through this, or will go through it? Since then, at any time, on any day, I often find myself asking: how many women are going through it *right now*?

AS I CONTEMPLATED WRITING THIS book, I looked up the statistics about abortion. As recently as 1992, 43% of all women would have had an abortion by the age of 45. By 2008, that number was down to 30% (still by the age of 45). These studies were both performed using CDC data. However, in their data collection methods, the CDC says that "states and areas voluntarily report data to the CDC for inclusion in its annual Abortion Surveillance Report. The CDC's Division of Reproductive Health prepares surveillance reports as data become available. There is no national requirement for data submission or reporting." This means that we may be looking at an incomplete picture. This is done under the guise of women's "right to privacy." In reality, keeping things taboo around abortion only further drives its stigma. This provides a ripe environment for state governments to tighten their hold around abortion rights.

Also excluded from this data are procedures that take place outside of licensed clinics, so-called "back alley abortions," and abortions performed via medication using the so-called abortion pill (Mifepristone and Misoprostol), which can now be obtained on the underground economy. If abortion were inexpensive and easy to obtain, these measures would be unnecessary. As it stands today, they continue to happen, and continue to remain mostly untraceable for researchers to include in their sources. Not to mention that procedures done outside of a medical clinic can be dangerous to women because of less-than ideal hygiene, tools, and training.

I continued to look for more recent and complete data, and found the Guttmacher Institute, a non-profit research institution whose data claims to be more comprehensive "than state and federal government sources." Their data is more complete because Guttmacher surveys every known abortion provider in the US every three years, and their data is ahead of the CDC, often by a year. Some states, like California, do not report their numbers to the CDC, and yet they report to Guttmacher. Their data cites that today's rate of abortion is down to 24% by the age of 45.

Comparing these data sets—CDC and Guttmacher—will not yield accurate results. As I got further into my research, I found these types of differences could leave room for interpretation and bending of data. Studies take time, and so they can lag behind data collection by a considerable margin, and research methods are inconsistent between reporting houses. This is not to say that we don't have a clear picture of abortion trends in our country. It reminds me a bit of climate change models: we can't say specifically which mote of dust will result in a cloud, but the research allows us to understand the problem in broad strokes. Abortion research cannot predict which individual woman will terminate an unintentional pregnancy, but we know with complete certainty that some will.

The last thing I want to be is a source of confusion on a well-researched but complex topic. Looking at the topic from a high level, we have a relatively accurate picture of abortion trends in the United States, but it would be remiss of us to believe that these numbers can fully capture what abortion looks like in *real life*. Data cannot capture the emotional turmoil a woman faces or the obstacles that will be a part of her path regardless of her decision. We live in a world where back alley abortions still happen; where some women traverse state lines to have a safe procedure; and where who knows how many children are born to mothers who might have chosen a different life altogether. As for what a typical scenario for a woman in the US who wants an abortion might look like, the following passage is based on my research to-date.

A few days or weeks after her period is due, the woman in our story realizes she hasn't begun to menstruate. Maybe she is on birth control, maybe she isn't. Statistically speaking, she's young, from a racial minority group, and there is a good chance she has a child at home already. After taking a home pregnancy test—she likely won't take the time off work to see a doctor—she confirms she is pregnant. She looks up an abortion clinic, goes on her day off work, but is surprised to find that she's at a pro-life clinic, masquerading as a place that performs abortions. After all, for each abortion care center in the US there are five fake clinics. She leaves, still determined to get an abortion, still having told no one in her inner circle she's pregnant.

She does more research, finds a real abortion clinic, but because there are so few in her state, she has to drive several hours. She can only get an appointment during work hours, so she takes precious time off—time she can't really financially afford. At the appointment they inform her that she can't have an abortion today—there is a waiting period, and she'll have to go home and wait 48 hours before she can schedule an actual procedure. The price? A little over $500, close to a month's rent for her. At this point she still hasn't told her boyfriend, though she has confided in some close girlfriends. It takes her six weeks of working extra hours and borrowing money from friends, but finally she has saved enough to have the procedure. When she calls to schedule an appointment the deathblow lands: she's too far along to have an abortion due to her state's individual regulations. At this point, it is inconceivable for her to drive to another state that might allow later term abortion, and so she tells her boyfriend, tells her family, and accepts her fate.

Along with whatever condemnation society and her family throw at her, the blame and shame for being irresponsible for becoming pregnant, and for even considering an abortion, lands squarely on her shoulders. Some men may attend doctor's appointments and, if women are lucky, help with costs and hold them through the hardest times. But in the end, we're the ones who ultimately live with the consequences—whatever those may be. Yes, men are a part of this story, but a story of abortion will always be a woman's story.

When we draw these composite sketches, it becomes too easy to forget that they are based on real people, living in the real world. People with unique concerns about their relationships, their bodies, their finances, and with individual aspirations for their lives. Each and every woman who chooses to have an abortion is entitled to be treated as herself, not to be simply seen as a statistic. Also worth noting here, is that in this memoir I will frequently discuss "women's" reproductive health, but it's important to remember that cis-gender women are not the only ones capable of becoming pregnant. The points I make also apply to transgender and non-binary individuals who, regardless of gender, possess a uterus and the related organs, and may therefore find themleves in a similar situation to mine.

Personally, I've learned more from living my version of this story than I have from 34 years of previous life experience. Surviving an emotional rock bottom will do that to a person; like the Dalai Lama says, "we find growth in the low places." I used to jump to quick judgment of myself and others, but my beliefs are more flexible now. I choose to think that people are probably trying their hardest in situations that look simple from the outside, but which are likely more challenging and nuanced for the person living them. I've realized that what I write today may not be true for me tomorrow, and that's okay. Better than okay, it's evidence of having learned something, and the amazing power of the human species to adapt as we go.

BUT WOULD I HAVE EVER chosen for this to be my story? Not in a million years. Never would I have wanted abortion to be my *thing*. In order to keep that softer mindset I spoke about before, to keep from mentally kicking myself for having gotten into this relationship, this pregnancy, this *situation* to begin with, I keep a picture of myself out on my bookshelf. In it, I'm about five or six. Blonde hair pulled back in a ponytail, bangs, sitting propped up on a pair of checkered pillows in the living room at my grandparent's house. The pillows are made of dark squares of smooth leather and light squares of suede that always felt cool to the touch. The picture was taken over spring break the year my brother had the chickenpox. When I look at that girl, at that innocent face and unburdened heart, I ask myself: *what would I want for her?*

In a perfect world, I'd love to see her go through life without so much as a single physical or emotional scratch. I'd like to see her carefree, doing meaningful work she's passionate about, where her self-esteem is based not on her looks but the shape of her heart, and where love is as honestly given to her as she decides to give it to others. But that's a pipe dream. We live in an unjust society, nestled within an ever-evolving planet, where life-altering events bring suffering every day. Given such uncertainty, I'd at least like to see that younger version of myself be treated with dignity and respect, and always given the benefit of the doubt. Most of all, I'd like her to love herself unconditionally, no matter what society says, and to know that she always has her own back.

I've had that picture on display ever since the abortion and now I think of her when I make decisions for myself. My life has changed so much since then, and the person I am today could not make the same choices now, beginning with the decision to date and stay in a relationship with a man like the broker. The writing of this book has reminded me why I made the decision I did, and it has given me a chance to marvel at the beauty of the life I have built as another burned itself to the ground. It has been hard yet healing work, and one of the most fulfilling endeavors of my life. I hope in reading my words, other women are reminded that their stories will look different one day, too. That however painful it might feel now, good can still come from their decision. I know the more open we can be with ourselves and others, and the more willing we are to share our truths, the better chance we will have to build the lives we are meant to live.

one

It was a punch to the gut every time he said it: *if you would just have an abortion*. The broker didn't want this child. Using his finely tuned negotiating skills, he was trying to bargain his way out of our situation. I could terminate the pregnancy now, and he'd freeze some sperm for me. He had already looked into the cost and the process, he said. Then, no matter what happened between the two of us, I'd have the assurance of having a child with a man whose history I knew, whenever I was ready. This way, I'd get the baby I wanted, and he'd be released from any obligation. I stood there, trying to process his logic. *What?*

I watched him as he tried to find the words to explain this to me. He always had the same look when he was pensive: face tilted up and to the right, eyes gazing in the same direction. His tongue would cover his upper lip while he thought. I had always found that look adorable. Not today. Finally, he told me that it was all about the circumstances. He had contributed in the making of this child, and so there was no way he could back out of the responsibility of caring for it. However, if I were to opt to have a child of his later, using his frozen sperm, then it would not be his doing, and he would feel no obligation to take care of it. *How completely absurd.*

We were standing at the far end of the parking lot of my gynecologist's office, traffic whizzing by on the other side of a mauve stuccoed wall. It was hot outside but there was a breeze in the air. Standing in the shade provided by giant eucalyptus trees, the wind on the back of my neck, we lingered for a while to talk. I was four weeks and a couple of days along and we had spent the past hour with the Physician's Assistant I normally saw for my annual exams. We were shown into the room, and I sat fully clothed and upright in a chair instead of taking the normal "position" in the stirrups. Looking at the exam table the idea of stirrups became warped in my mind, like a word you say too many times in a row. There was no ultrasound, no fetal heart rate, just a list of do's and don'ts. No to alcohol or soft cheeses, and only one cup of coffee per day. Yes to prenatal vitamins.

I had been seeing the same PA, Meghan, for a couple of years. That day her carefully chosen words and blank affect conveyed that she understood this must have been an unplanned pregnancy. The broker was visibly nervous—out of character for him—and was trying to be humorous. At one point he made a comment about not knowing my last name. Meghan and I stared at him blankly. It wasn't until we were walking outside after the appointment that the broker explained he was trying to joke that he and I had had a one-night stand. *Funny*, I responded, deadpan. Through our discomfort, Meghan remained stoic and compassionate. Without expressing to her that I wanted to keep the pregnancy and the broker did not, I asked about "other options" as I'd promised him I would. She said she'd had plenty of patients terminate pregnancies, and that at this stage there was nothing more inside me than "a blob of cells."

A blob of cells that I already related to as a child. I'd spent a lot of time looking in the mirror in the few days since I'd found out I was pregnant—not something I do often. I wanted to watch myself become a mother. I'd stand in the bathroom at work and look in my hazel eyes and wonder about the life to come. Would I have a daughter? Would she have my eyes? I'd put my hands on my abdomen when no one was looking and wonder what a pregnant belly would look like on my frame. It was way too early for that—there was nothing to feel and certainly no movement—but it was there, and it was mine, and I loved the alone time I had already shared with that child. Now, I was torn.

My relationship with the broker was crumbling and we were fighting constantly. In my soul I knew that if we did this, it would be as co-parents. The idea saddened me. I had grown up with loving parents who were committed to family life and who had, by then, celebrated more than 35 years together. I knew that marriages had both good and bad, highs and lows, but I was so grateful for the stability and love that I had been raised with. I was sad for myself to know that I would have to give up that future, but mostly I was concerned that I could only foresee an acrimonious co-parenting situation. I imagined cold, business-like phone calls discussing schedules, and waiting in the car while my child walked into his home, a curt nod of the broker's head as he shut the door.

And what would single motherhood be like? I thought about where I could get an apartment close to my work. Could my mom help out? Or would I have to get a nanny? What if the broker had a revolving door of wives and girlfriends like his brothers? If it was a boy, what behavior would he model to him? Worse, what if it was a girl? Would she expect to be treated the way he treated most women? The way he treated me? Was I going to be tied to that man, forever? With nearly every other choice in life, there is a way out, an escape hatch. But once you have a child with someone, they are in your life no matter what (or if not, resentment will fill their place). The physical nature of the pregnancy brought that home to me. This was permanent.

I abandoned those thoughts and brought my mind back to the present moment, back to the parking lot where I was standing, crying. I didn't understand his logic. We had conceived a child already, our potential future as co-parents already growing inside me. If he didn't want to be a father now, why would he feel any differently later?

The sun was slowly sinking, and we were no longer shaded by the trees. The summer heat dried my tears nearly as fast as they fell on his shirt. In this moment he was both my shelter and my storm, and for as much as I didn't want to stay, I didn't believe that I had the courage or strength to leave, either.

THE YEAR BEFORE I'D MET the broker, I'd been all set to move to a small town where I had found myself in a relationship with an old roommate, a man I call the engineer. On a visit to the area, he offered me a place to stay. We laughed the whole weekend. And we discovered that for the first time in our lives, we were both single at the same time. Sparks flew.

After we were established as a couple, my friends all commented that I seemed singularly happy with this guy. It was true. We climbed mountains together, went on vacations, and eventually began to talk about the life we wanted to build together. We'd been friends for nine years by the time we started dating; we had each other figured out completely. We even looked alike—both tall and lean, tan from so many miles in the sun. We were headed down the same path, except for one sticking point: children. He already had a child from a previous relationship and was hesitant about having more. I loved the idea of being close with his son, but I knew I wanted a child of my own as well.

I had always wanted to be a mother and had gone through life assuming the pieces would fall into place over time. The women in my maternal line have always considered themselves late bloomers—my great grandmother married at the age of 25, back in 1911, and at that time she was considered quite the spinster. In 1952 her daughter, my grandmother, had her last child at the age of 42, which is considered a geriatric pregnancy even by today's standards, and was definitely abnormal back then. Given my family history of late pregnancies, it didn't seem much of a concern to me when my early relationships didn't end with marriage and children. Around 33 that began to change, and my laissez-faire attitude about starting a family shifted. I found myself hurt with each new pregnancy in my friend group, shying away from cards that looked like they might be birth announcements, and always keeping a close eye on women at parties to see who wasn't drinking.

As I watched my cousins and friends enter the foreign and vulnerable world of first-time parenthood—showing up to my cousin's house and her opening the door with her one-year-old son in her arms or arriving at a girlfriend's house to see a tiny table painted gold and set for a tea party—I found myself longing to look into the eyes of a baby the way they did and know that it was mine. I could picture a kid with ears that stick out just a little too much, and a cowlick on her forehead that never quite lays flat. I wanted to be the source of comfort and laughter for a small life; to watch the development of a personality all its own. I knew that having kids was a relationship deal-breaker for me, and over the course of months this difference between the engineer and I crystallized into an unspoken rift. Eventually, I began to resent what felt like his denial of my desire to be a parent. When he asked if I thought his son looked like him, it was a lightning bolt shot straight through me. We were at his home, him sitting at a counter stool while I was at the long kitchen table. He turned the phone screen towards me, his face excited and eager, betraying his desire to have me respond with, "Yes, he does look like you." I finished the statement in my mind, *and like his mother*. I realized I had to choose: a life with this wonderful man and his child or leave and potentially start a family of my own. I left.

Historically, I've always taken plenty of time to be alone after a breakup, finding solace and eventually pleasure in the time by myself. But this breakup was somehow different. Because I'd had feelings for this man for so long, and because he had become in my mind the very definition of a perfect partner—kind, handsome, successful—my heartbreak was deep. It was impossible for me to imagine ever loving someone else, hard to imagine even wanting to. That said, having drawn such a hard line in the sand about wanting a family, I had a sense of urgency about moving forward toward that end. Three months after the breakup, I got on a dating app for the first time ever. In short order, I met the broker.

We seemed like a great match. We were both progressing steadily along the career path. He had a super sweet Labradoodle, Chloe, and I loved dogs. He was a rock climber; I was a trail runner. Later, we discovered we were friends of friends after all, as we knew a few people in common through those communities. For our first date, we met at a coffee shop and sat on a patio. A young woman with a puppy sat next to us and we spent the next 45 minutes oohing and ahhing over the little guy. The broker tentatively asked me if I'd care to go to lunch with him, and I was delighted at the offer. On our walk over to the restaurant, he commented on my height—that I hadn't lied about being 5'10" in my profile—and I remember thinking I liked his sweater. Turns out I'd spend the better part of the next eight months sleeping in it.

The subject of relationship deal-breakers came up early. At the time, he was considering opening his own brokerage in Georgia, nearer to his sister. I told him I wouldn't leave the southwestern US. I asked him about his own deal-breakers; knowing he was a year and a half out of a divorce, he must have some. He wanted a family. Reflecting back on my memory of the night, I don't remember him even looking at me when he said that. We were on a last dog-walk of the night and he was recounting to me that he'd dated several older women before me, and while they were more "mature" than women our age, none of them seemed to want children. I shook off his perspective about women's maturity at different points in our lives and left the conversation satisfied that we had similar life goals. After the collapse of my last relationship, I'd promised myself to stay away from men who didn't want children. The broker definitely ticked that box.

Not too long after that night, I was walking him to his car in my apartment complex. We were both lingering, not ready for the night to end. Holding one another and rocking back and forth, my face buried in his neck, we talked about children. He joked that we should hope any child of ours would end up with his ears and my math skills. I barked out a sharp laugh. It felt like my heart swelled in my chest at the mention of family. It straightened my spine and pulled me up to give him a kiss on the cheek while my own face was split with a smile.

BUT THEN THE CRACKS REALLY began to show. One day at work the broker texted me to comment on the success of his Fantasy Basketball team. It had been a busy day, and I rocked back in my chair, the message a welcome relief from the project management program on my screen. He'd sent over a screenshot of his leaderboard. His avatar caught my eye: a Lakers' cheerleader with her breasts mostly exposed. Her face was out of the shot, the bottom of her very large bosom pushing out of a jersey that was pulled up to nipple height. The top of a tan stomach was barely visible. My heart rate jumped through the roof and my breath caught in my throat. I pushed backward in my chair as though to get away from my phone. I locked the screen immediately afraid a coworker might walk around the corner and see her. I had a good girlfriend in the office, and I walked over to her desk to see what she made of it. When she looked, her eyebrows went up and her eyes grew wide. *No way*, she said, her face stern. *Bad news.*

After work the broker and I met at an apartment complex not far from where I was living at the time—my lease was up shortly and I was looking for a new place. He had offered to go with me as a second set of eyes. During the showing, things were tense between us. Once we were back at our cars we were finally able to speak freely. Neither of us raised our voices during the ensuing conversation, but we each held steadfast to our ground as we aired our opinions. I asked him about other men who played in the league; what were their avatars? Jerseys, mostly. *Boring*, he said. I kept pushing; isn't the objectification of women disrespectful? What did it mean for me? Was I supposed to look like her? I could feel hot anger rising up the middle of my chest as I said this. My body shifted as my shoulders squared to face him and my energy filled the space between us. My last question lingered in the air, the expression on my face driving the point home. He held my gaze for a minute, but then blinked, and relented. He was afraid we'd gone too far down a rabbit hole. That bickering like this wasn't really "us." He asked if I wanted to have dinner together after this, and I dropped the topic. He never changed the avatar.

It was the first in a series of incidents that shifted the balance of our relationship, and my trust in him began to erode. There was that time he lied about cheating on an ex. And another. His admission that he was once addicted to porn. When I first began to spend the night, he'd push things further between us physically, backing me into the corner of saying "no, not tonight" multiple times. When we finally did have sex, he said it was about time; *he wasn't just running a bed and breakfast here.* He called me uptight because I liked to sleep clothed. If I expressed any doubts about his conduct, this would be reflected back as me overreacting, my own insecurities, with him assuming the role of the wrongly accused.

Over the course of a couple of months, a fog descended around me. His reasoning seemed so logical when we were together, but left me doubting when I thought back on the incidents or told my friends about them. These moments were like the occasional pothole in an altogether nice road: I overlooked them and kept on driving. Now, I cringe at how easily I was manipulated. But with gaslighting, the whole point is that you can't detect when it's happening.

Everything logical in me was saying to give him the benefit of the doubt. My journals read like a tennis match between my intuition and his voice, speaking from a place inside me: *I don't trust him (not sure if I should). But you want to be in a relationship that's going somewhere. I don't think he is the right person for me. But you love him.* The emotional side of myself was soft and questioning; the logical side, represented by his voice, was firm and factual just like the broker himself. That voice brought up evidence of him being a good boyfriend—like the time when I was sick and he wasn't sure which soup to bring me, so he stopped at two of my favorite restaurants and brought home soup from each. That voice reminded me how much he did for me—like taking up running even though he hated it, just to spend more time with me. That voice reminded me that he wanted kids, and that I'd left another relationship to pursue starting a family of my own. So I continued to listen to *that voice*. I told myself that we'd just continue dating for the time being, to see where it went. We weren't ready to marry or have kids anyway—I still had an escape hatch. But a little while came and went, and soon enough I had a boyfriend. Meanwhile, for the first time in my adult life, I was sexually active while not taking hormonal birth control.

MY HISTORY WITH THE PILL started in high school, long before sex was on my radar as a possibility or even an interest. I was taking it as a requirement of another medication that had the potential to cause birth defects. It was years until I got to college and had my first serious boyfriend, and by then I thought it just made sense to stay on it. At the time, I didn't stop to question why it was a foregone conclusion that birth control was my responsibility; I just knew that I didn't want to become pregnant and I trusted myself to be consistent about it more than I did an 18-year-old dude. Since my mom and most of the women in my family seemed to get pregnant with no problem, I was religious about setting an alarm on my watch—and later my watch *and* my phone—to ensure that not one little white pill was missed.

Throughout college, and for more than a decade after, I maintained the practice of using some kind of hormonal birth control. Finally, after so many years of responsibility, I became exhausted by the burden and generally disillusioned with the idea that this should always be my responsibility to bear. So it came to be that a couple of months prior to dating the engineer, I stopped, and was happy to give my body a much-needed reset. I was single and I figured it would be nice to take a break from the nightly alarms that had been a staple in my life for so long.

The first month, I noticed my body change in so many ways. Initially I put on weight (five pounds was nearly enough to send me scurrying back to my pills), but then the weight came off, and an extra five pounds with it. Some spots on my skin that I thought were sun damage gently faded away. I had never considered myself particularly moody, but still I noticed a smoothing of my overall emotional state—there were still highs and lows, but it was a much gentler switch from one to the other. I was markedly less irritated by the everyday annoyances of life. How much had this medication influenced the woman I had been for nearly two decades? Did I even know the *real me* or had she been obscured all along? In a larger context, I found myself wondering to what extent has this "miracle" pill shaped all of our lives?

By the time the broker and I had "the talk," I was pretty opposed to going back on hormonal birth control. Between the weight loss and the gentler moods, being off hormones seemed like a win/win situation for me. He didn't seem too phased by the idea of using condoms. So I was surprised when one day he made an offhand comment that "sex with condoms is lame." I filed it away as something to remember and be aware of, but I never felt like it was aimed at me or that it was intended as an attempt to change our birth control routine.

Between the comment about the condoms, my own journal entries, and the slow erosion of my trust, I'm surprised now that I didn't more quickly follow my intuition that this guy was bad news. I was like a pilot hellbent on getting to my destination: I just kept flying, turning off warning lamps one by one as they came on. My destination? A life in which family was a primary feature. I'm sure biology played some role here—the good old ticking clock. But it was becoming increasingly painful for me to see each of my friends marching steadily along with their children—first in preschool, then kindergarten, beginning to take the training wheels off bikes, learning to swim. My life seemed so desperately far from that picture, and if motherhood was the passport to happiness, then the broker seemed like the ticket.

FAST FORWARD TO THE ONE-YEAR mark after the abortion. I began to spend a lot of time thinking about the circumstances of my pregnancy and how it compared to what it might be like for other women who are trying, or not, to conceive. In the past handful of years, as many of my friends became mothers, it seemed like just as many had struggled to become pregnant. Several couples I knew had spent the GDP of a small island nation on IVF treatments. Some had even considered taking an extended leave to go to South Africa for six weeks where there are top-notch private fertility clinics. Along with the expertise of those doctors, the procedure is a fraction of the cost it is here in the US.

Listening to these stories, I felt at once great empathy for my friends, and positively treacherous for having had an abortion. I know those women would have given just about anything to get pregnant as easily as I did. I vividly remember a conversation with a friend who'd been having a particularly long and trying road to pregnancy. We were on the phone the night before she was leaving for a backpacking trip in the Tetons. She updated me about where she was at in her fertility journey, I told her stories about my new life in California, and she laughed, *thank goodness you didn't stay with the broker. Can you imagine if you guys had actually had kids together!* I was silent for a beat and then went on to comment how happy I was to be away from him. A lie of omission. The first and only friend I hadn't been honest with.

There was a knot in my stomach for the rest of our conversation. I wanted so badly to tell her what an amazing mother she'd be. I wanted to tell her how much I wanted to have a child myself, with the right man. I wanted to rage with her against the misfortune that I should have gotten pregnant at a time when she could not. I wanted to explain to her how careful I had been for 17 years, and how unfair it felt to find myself in the situation I did after one careless month. But instead, I kept my mouth shut. Maybe we would get there one day.

As hard as it is for some women to become pregnant, unintended pregnancies also happen all the time. In 2001, 48% of all pregnancies in the US were unintended. That figure rose to 51% in 2008 and dropped back to 45% in 2011. I was blown away when I read that. Consistently, half of all pregnancies are unintentional. Just let that sink in for a moment. When I first read this statistic, I was so overwhelmed by it that I immediately reached for my phone, *who could I tell this crazy thing I just learned?* In the end I didn't call anyone but ruminated on how many lives are upended by this experience. Over time, it gave me a little perspective about my own pregnancy and eased my feeling of guilt with my friends who couldn't conceive. Clearly, I wasn't the only one this was happening to, and maybe, I wasn't to blame.

In the US, there is this feeling that birth control is something we have *all figured out*. That it is 100% effective, and we all know how to use it correctly, and we all do that all the time. But if the preceding statistic tells us anything, it's that birth control is not all figured out. Birth control is still considered a woman's responsibility, but it's a burden that we don't always want to carry. Besides which, it doesn't always work. The pill comes in at 91% effective (99% if taken perfectly, though most women fall short of that), the shot 94% effective, and IUDs and sterilization are still not perfect—both are 99% effective.

The other staggering number to take into consideration in all of this, is that women tend to live at the intersection of being both sexually active and fertile for a full 30 years. As a woman, you worry about pregnancy from the time of your first sexual encounter until menopause. Your options should you become pregnant—motherhood or abortion—are weighty enough without the added stigma around ending an unplanned and/or unwanted pregnancy.

What toll does that level of subconscious worry take? One time in college, I received a failing grade on a Physics exam. I was devastated, and immediately set up an appointment with the professor to see what we could do about my future in the class. At that point in my life, school was everything, and the thought of not passing a class was unbearable. In the four days I had to wait before our appointment, I was a wreck—anxious, unable to focus, and with absolutely no appetite. When you have that much strain on you, it can become difficult to complete even the simplest tasks. There is a lot I want to do in this life, a lot that I think needs to be done. But how much of the time do we spend preoccupied with the question: *what happens if I get pregnant?* How much of my energy and focus was caught up with this worry? Women represent 50% of the population. Imagine how much collective headspace we could free up if birth control was not our sole responsibility, and if abortion was not so taboo.

As for the broker and I, we responsibly used condoms for the first several months of our relationship—it wasn't like we threw caution to the wind immediately. But one night, he asked if we could skip it *just this once.* The conversation came up in bed, as he was getting frisky with me. It made me uneasy. He promised that he knew his body well and that he wouldn't mess it up. I held off that first night, but as the topic came up again I eventually relented. The first time he pulled out, it was nerve wracking, but it seemed to go well. The next time I was a bit more relaxed about the whole thing, and it was then that he changed the rules of the game—he surprised me at the last second. I ran to the bathroom in a panic. When I returned to the bedroom I rocked back and forth on the edge of the bed, feeling the beginnings of anxiety prickling my skin. I've always been quite high strung, the broker in every way my opposite. He grew up in a small beach community and couldn't be bothered to get upset about nearly anything. This was no different. He rolled onto his side to face me and said, *Well baby, I guess we just rolled the dice.* I retorted, *We? Where was I in this decision?* He laughed good-naturedly at my worry and tried to pull me into an embrace.

I can't recall the latter part of that night. Did I sleep in his arms? My unease about the relationship was growing by then, and I often spent nights at the edge of his king-sized bed, facing the window, sleeplessly staring at the outside light spilling in around the edges of the black-out curtains. The next day I had to take a work trip, and by the time I was on the plane I had decided to take Plan B as soon as we touched down. I texted the broker to let him know. I still have a screenshot of his reply: *I know I'm not always as sensitive as you want or need, I'll work on it. I think I'm not stressed because of everyone I've dated I think having a child with you would be the easiest. As in I think we would agree on a lot and have similar values. So yes, I would prefer to continue to get there if we get there but an "oops" with you isn't the end of times in my mind.* I took the pill and got on with my work.

THE FOLLOWING MONTH HE "SURPRISED" me again. We were out of town for a friend's birthday along with several other couples. Kait wanted to escape the heat, and spend her 30th away from the city, in the mountains. She rented a big house for all of us—the group consisted of Kait and her husband, the broker and I, another girl-friend Kait and I shared in common, and one other couple. The broker and I had an upstairs bedroom to ourselves that overlooked the backyard where there was a large garden, a brick oven for pizzas, and a hot tub. The final night we were there, the broker and I snuck upstairs early for some alone time, which turned into us fooling around. By this point we'd had unprotected sex a few times, but he was good about pulling out—I had been so upset the one time he hadn't, that he seemed to get the message. That night, he didn't. Afterward, I ran to the bathroom angry and near tears, trying to be quiet and fast while awkwardly jumping up and down in an attempt to rid myself of the unwanted surprise. *Oh please body, help me out here.*

The next morning, we drove home through one of the worst hail-storms of my life. I remember that drive so clearly: the sound of the hail hitting the car was explosive and so loud we could barely talk. The broker's dog Chloe was cowering in the backseat, and the windshield wipers were completely ineffective and unable to keep up. The broker was driving and we were unsure about the best course of action. Try to stay on the road, creeping forward? Or pull over and hope we wouldn't be rear-ended by a car that was attempting to follow us. Hunkered down in the passenger seat, worried about making the wrong decision, I closed my fingers around my ears to shut out the apocalypse outside. Never once on that drive did the broker and I discuss the incident, nor did I feel a pang of fear that I might become pregnant. When the storm finally passed, the rest of the drive was uneventful and the mood quiet between us in the car.

Looking back, I wonder what was different that time than the month before. Why didn't I immediately go scurrying for Plan B? Perhaps because I was excited and preoccupied about a coming vacation that week. And although the logic is skewed, I think the effectiveness of Plan B the previous month lulled me into a false sense of security. It made it seem like not using birth control was no big deal. Back at home from Kait's birthday, I went about packing my car for the road trip I was headed out on. I was making a big loop of the Southwest—to see friends, get out in nature, and do a little mountain biking along the way. I knew things with the broker weren't working, and I was looking forward to some space to make a decision about us. I meticulously packed my gear, lined up time with friends, and checked my car was in good shape: oil change, tire rotation, emergency gear. Unbeknownst to me, my body was quietly busy splitting cells, making space, getting ready to incubate a new life.

TWO AND A HALF WEEKS later I arrived home exhausted from driving, but mentally fresh from the time away. I had made some major decisions while I was on the road—I had called my job, letting them know I was leaving. I got paperwork in motion to move out of my apartment. I was lining everything up for a move out of state, I just had to rip the band-aid off and tell the broker.

We spent time together that evening and he was the best version of himself: kind and caring. When I told him I wanted to leave Arizona he said he was committed to making things work between us. I realized then that there was no easy way out of this relationship for me; I'd have to be direct, be strong, and leave. Breaking up with someone is the worst—you know there is something better out there, but first you have to survive the heartache. And when you are the one doing the leaving, it almost feels like you are choosing to break your own heart.

The next morning I was pacing in his living room, having spent the night. My stomach was a knot of nerves and my legs too antsy to sit still. I hadn't quite figured out the words to end it. I knew he was wrong for me, but I also knew he'd keep trying to convince me otherwise. I needed willpower and I needed my wits about me. He was getting ready to go climb, and while I was waiting for him to pack his things I began to mindlessly scroll Instagram for a few minutes.

The day before, in his endeavor to show me how great we were together, he had asked to follow me on the app. I had said yes, and requested to follow him as well. This morning was the first time I had checked out his photos. It seemed only natural to also take a look at who he followed. I clicked the little button, saw the list pop up, and scrolled. At first, the results confused me. When I realized what I was looking at my blood pressure skyrocketed. The avatars for the accounts were mostly women with very little clothing on, immediately bringing me back to our conversation about the Laker's cheerleader. It seemed his porn addiction had morphed into an *Insta*-porn addiction. I had no idea this sub-culture existed and was shocked to see this content on such a widely available app. I clicked on an account or two and was met by an endless stream of women in provocative poses wearing nearly nothing, and sometimes, depending on the pose, actually nude. By now I could feel my heart beating *hard* in my chest. I took a few deep breaths to compose myself. This was actually good, I told myself, this would strengthen my resolve to leave him. It was the final straw.

Needless to say, we fought. The words "it's over" were never actually spoken, but I left his house with a slammed door and no intention to return. Again he called me names—prude, uptight—and tried to shift the conversation to why his behavior was normal and mine was not. But we had come too far, and I could see what he was really all about. I'd finally hit my limit.

On the drive home, I called my brother and told him it was over. He was proud of me. In my apartment I tried to read but couldn't quite focus. I puttered around on my phone aimlessly for a few minutes, scrolling past the different icons on my home screen. One app caught my eye. Flo, a bright pink app with a feather on it. A menstrual tracker that I had started using only a few months before. It jogged my memory that my period was supposed to start on Saturday. *But it was Sunday.* I'd had particularly bad cramps when I was on the last leg of my drive home, but that was common for me right before my period started. I was usually regular but being a day late, or even two, wasn't out of the question for me. I remembered something else from my drive—my breasts had been sore. In the car, I assumed that I just had sore pectorals from all the mountain biking I'd been doing. Now, I realized that had never happened to me before either, and I had been biking for the better part of a decade. Refocusing on my screen, I clicked on the app. Sure enough, I was a day late.

I walked to my bathroom and took a pregnancy test out of the cabinet—just one. It was years old and had come in a two pack that I'd bought while I was with another boyfriend. Everything about that time was different. We'd been using birth control, he went with me to buy the test, and if it had been positive we knew we'd keep it. But that was not the situation today. I went to the bathroom alone, and unwrapped the test. The package was so innocuous. The shape of the test and the wrapper reminded me of the little glow sticks I'd used when scuba diving at night—the ones you crack open and shake to illuminate. It felt so innocent, and yet the stakes were anything but. So many women's lives altered forever; a baby when you don't want one, no baby when you do. I unwrapped the package to see what my fortune would be today.

IT WASN'T SUPPOSED TO HAPPEN that fast. The test was supposed to take two minutes. But the moment the liquid hit the paper, the little pink lines appeared. I was pregnant. I re-read the instructions just to be safe—did two lines really mean pregnant? Or was it one? A minute ago I could have sworn it was two, but now I couldn't be certain, or maybe I didn't want to be. The box indicated two lines meant pregnant. I looked back over at the test. Two lines. Not even 15 seconds must have elapsed. How was that possible? The instructions clearly stated that you had to wait two minutes. Two minutes, two lines. I wanted those minutes back.

I don't know how I made it from the bathroom to the living room floor, but one second I was perched on the edge of the tub, staring in disbelief as the test results flashed in neon before my eyes, and the next moment I was on the living room floor gasping for breath in a grotesque parody of child's pose. The carpet was grainy on my knees and the smell of dust reached my nose. *Breathe. Just make your diaphragm work. Get some oxygen into your lungs.* Minutes passed. I was a fish out of water. I tried sitting up, opening my chest to try to gain a physical advantage over the air I could barely coax into my lungs.

I was pregnant.

Shock kept my mind from moving any further. I stared at my houseplants taking in the morning sun on the north wall of my living room. It was utterly silent in the room. The rise and fall of the emotion from the initial test result left me reeling, the inside of my mind quiet like the room around me. My life was forever changed, and yet when I looked around the room, everything remained the same. How is that possible? Time passed. How long had I been sitting there? Minutes? Hours?

As my mind came back to my body, thoughts began to creep back in. Slowly at first, but after a few minutes they raced towards me hot and chaotic. This can't be happening to me. How is this real? When did it happen? No. NO. I need to take another test. Do I have another test? Am I sure I was supposed to get my period today? Or yesterday? I should check my app again.

I have to tell the broker.

Oof. There it was. I knew I had to tell him, but I didn't want to face that truth. It felt like such a cosmic betrayal that at the moment when I really felt like I was pulling my life together, fate conspired to pull it apart again.

I knew the broker was out climbing, but I called his phone anyway. No answer. I left a rare voicemail asking him to meet me at his place immediately. I grabbed my keys and drove the 20 minutes back to his house. Once there, I paced, trying in vain to quiet my mind. My thoughts were too frantic to let my body sit still. As soon as I saw him walking up the front path I stepped towards him. He was scowling. I wasn't ready. I turned my back to him for just another second, trying to gain composure over myself.

He reached the door and unlocked it, not meeting my eyes. He let me in, and I told him before he had a chance to shut the door. No greeting, no hug. No two minutes for him either. His jaw fell open, his eyes scanned back and forth, almost as though they were chasing the thoughts in his head. He hugged me, hard, for a full minute, perhaps because by then I was sobbing, or perhaps because he needed the comfort himself. Then he maneuvered past me and sprawled, king-like on the couch—torso back, legs open in a wide V, arms out to either side. The look on his face said it all. Utter disbelief.

two

Let's get this nightmare over with.

My friend Laura used these exact words to describe her frame of mind when she was about to get an abortion. At age 19, having an affair with her boss (who had a girlfriend), broke and underemployed, she was the only woman I'd heard speak openly about her abortion *before* I told her about my own. The first time she told me we were on a hike and I was caught off guard when she said it. As the conversation went on, I realized it must be scary to tell someone that, and I was grateful that she trusted me. Laura and I met in college, both of us in our late 20s by then. She was on the triathlon team and was getting high marks in all of her engineering classes. Upon graduation she passed a notoriously difficult exam to become a professional engineer. She loved the outdoors and was a dog owner like I was. We were so alike, and at that age I still couldn't imagine either of us getting pregnant, let alone having an abortion. Her confession surprised me, but beyond that initial conversation, I never gave her story more than a passing thought—never assumed I would find myself in the same situation. Until I did. When I was trying to make the decision whether or not to keep the pregnancy, I recalled her words.

More than a year after my own abortion, I was vacationing in Colorado when we met up for a few days. Her company was working on a project in a small mountain town and they had set her up in a condo there. On a break between jobs, I wanted to take the opportunity to see her while I could and was happy to use that as an excuse to get to the mountains. My first night in town we went to a Vietnamese restaurant where all the windows were steamed up against the chilly weather outside. It was fall, and in the mountains, cold weather starts early in the season. It was dark outside when we met and we sat at the bar where we warmed up with steaming hot cups of tea before we ate. The place was quiet, the muffled conversations around us creating a sense of intimacy.

Laura was newly married with two step kids, and I asked her about family life. She checked in about my father, who had been diagnosed with Alzheimer's several years before. The conversation turned to her abortion not long after that. Now that I had been through the experience myself, I wanted to hear her story again.

Laura was gentle when she began to answer my questions, but being herself, she couldn't help but rib me about some parts of both of our stories. She is hands down the funniest friend I have and the laughter had a calming effect on me that night. I had been a little shaky from anxiety but I became still and quiet as she spoke, totally caught up in what she was telling me. Her circumstances were so different than mine—I could see why, at age 19, the decision felt like a foregone conclusion. Unlike me, she never worried that this might be her only shot at being a mother, considered what a co-parenting situation might look like, or the specific implications of being a single mom and the family breadwinner. She knew she didn't want to have a child so young, when she had so much she still wanted to do with her life.

I don't envy any woman faced with electing to have an abortion, but I wish it had been that black and white for me. In the days and weeks after I found out I was pregnant, my thoughts were all over the place: initially I wanted to keep it, then as things became more complicated I was ambivalent, swinging wildly back and forth between keeping the baby and terminating the pregnancy. I don't like emotional *messiness*. I find scattered, competing thoughts uncomfortable and grasping. I wanted a clear-cut decision, with easy steps I could follow to get things *back to normal*.

IF I'D HAVE KNOWN SOMEDAY that I'd be able to look back at my own story without wincing in pain, I may have been able to laugh at the broker's reaction the day we found out. His initial way of denying the plain truth was to have me take test after test, hoping that *just one* might come back negative. After about the fourth test, I wondered out loud what he would have done had five come back positive and one negative. *Trust the negative one*, he shrugged.

We had come to an emotional detente that morning after I broke the news. I didn't think that I could handle the situation alone, and the broker had wanted us to stay together anyway. We spent the day together but avoided the topic of the Instagram accounts, and instead focused on the matter at hand. That evening, we walked our normal route with Chloe, taking twice as long as usual, letting her meander around the yards and flower beds while our thoughts and emotions took similar winding paths. It was so much to take in. I stayed the night that night, though neither of us slept much. We'd periodically reach out to one another, not saying anything but acknowledging the other's presence with a stroke of the back here, a brush of the hair there. The bedroom felt so quiet and still, like a universe unto itself. I wished we could stay there, frozen in time, the world unchanged. I anchored myself to him that night, appreciative of his warmth and the illusion of safety I found in his arms. The spell was broken with the rising sun.

The broker called me on the drive into work that morning, a Monday. We'd parted just moments before, him rushing out the door to make it in on time, me taking the dog for another walk before she was in for the day. I was surprised and relieved to see his name pop up on my phone. I didn't want to be alone, either, and hearing his voice soothed me a bit, the singsong rhythm of his words in his resonant baritone. Knowing that we were in this together took the edge off my own anxiety. At some point during the call, I commented that he seemed so cool and nonplussed by the whole thing. He gave a snort of laughter. If that was the case, how come he was calling me just 15 minutes after he'd left the house?

I was talking over my Airpods and kept glancing to the east, the sun coming up over a nearby mountain range painting the sky orange. I knew those mountains well, from so many runs and bike rides through them. I pictured him in his suit and tie, driving his sleek black sedan to his downtown office. We led such different lives. When we had first begun dating it seemed like we had so much in common—similar career trajectories, desires for a family—like we were on the same path. Time had revealed this not to be true. Our values were completely at odds, and when truly faced with the prospect of a family the broker was clearly not interested, or at the very least, not ready. *How are we going to make this work?* He didn't have any better ideas than I did.

Our situation was complicated, yes, but it wasn't a total nightmare. A bit of a mess? For sure. I was pregnant by a man I'd been wanting to break up with for months. A man whose moral compass made him less than ideal "father material." Was I terrified? Of course. My life had taken a sharp turn off the clear, straight path that had stretched out in front of me, down a faded trail, deep into a shadowy wood. I had no idea what the following days and weeks held for my body, let alone the balance of my life. I clung to the hope that since we were both well-educated grown-ups, we would be reasonable enough to work this out, whatever "this" came to mean.

Looking back, our call that morning was like the first trickle of water that turns into a flash flood. One minute, life is moving at a steady pace, a slow-moving stream babbling merrily along, well contained within its banks. The next, it's impossible to see through the murk and debris to where the stream once was, as the very ground on which you were standing just moments earlier gets swept away in a swirling chaos of confusion and panic and fear.

AND THE WORLD CONTINUED TO turn, as if nothing had changed. Bills needed to be paid, work assignments completed, the refrigerator stocked. The initial shock had subsided, and the broker and I were going about our life as we had before. A few days after we'd gotten the news, we were at the grocery store, when I wandered to the vitamin aisle and browsed an impressive selection of prenatal options. We'd not yet been to visit my gynecologist, but I knew they were a must-have for pregnancy. The brightly colored bottles vied for my attention: Budget Friendly! All Natural! Household Brand! I'd actually taken prenatal vitamins for a while not too long after college because of their biotin content, hoping it would make my hair grow in thicker. I remember opening my medicine cabinet and looking at them, daydreaming of ultrasounds and swelling bellies and nurseries full of books. I knew I wanted to be a mother, but it was all a fantasy for the future built around a fairytale romance with Prince Charming. Now, here I was weighing the trade-off between a higher folic acid content and guaranteed vegetarian capsules. I went with the latter. Back at the cart, I tossed them in without thinking.

The broker gave me a look. *What?* I raised my eyebrows, genuinely confused. *Wasn't it a bit early for those?* he asked me. I reeled off what I knew about why it was actually quite important to begin taking them at the start of a pregnancy, as they could prevent neural tube defects like spina bifida and lower the chance of a miscarriage. I told him women should be taking them before pregnancy, so it was really important for me to get started right away. He continued to stare, deadpan. He was a professional negotiator and knew well how to wipe the emotion from his face. I pressed him to tell me what was up. *I don't think you should get the vitamins. If you start ... I mean ... I don't want you to get attached. If you're taking care of it, I'm afraid you'll be more likely to keep it.*

He was looking at the floor, unwilling to meet my eyes. His normally upright posture deflated. My heart broke then for both of us, and I felt my breath become shallow as I closed my eyes and absorbed the hurt. His posture was familiar. It was a vulnerable stance; he knew how upsetting that statement would be for me and wanted to guard me against the blow and to put himself in an easier light if I didn't agree with him. But it was his truth. A truth that would become our impasse, and that was playing out right here in some random Albertson's with the whole world watching and no one the wiser.

We continued filling up our cart with vegetables, cereal, the jasmine rice he couldn't seem to go a single meal without eating. An icy wall of silence slowly forming between us. I left the vitamins in the cart.

From there things steadily got worse. What had begun as a considerate conversation between friends disintegrated to a cold war. We could not agree on the best path forward. Every time we found a piece of neutral ground to stand on, another disagreement would raise its head and put each of us on the offensive again. How we would live; his attitude toward women; who would take care of the child; our income. The constant back and forth was exhausting, fraying my nerves like a gale force wind, whipping us this way and that, giving us a moment's rest only to blast us from another, unexpected, direction. I felt like I'd never be able to anchor myself to a clear picture of what our future together might look like.

As we began to realize the depth of our divide, it became evident that our relationship was unlikely to survive us having a child. Even as, in our increasingly panicked state, we each began to prepare for the possibility of parenthood.

FOR HIS PART, THE BROKER thought the best idea would be to invest in real estate. He had been considering buying for some time but had never acted on the impulse. It seemed like all of Phoenix was gentrifying, and he'd seen one of his brothers make solid returns on real estate. He'd also seen a coworker of his buy a modest home on the outskirts of a nice neighborhood and within three years of the purchase, his home value had increased by six figures. The potential of adding a child into the mix tipped the scales on the broker's decision-making process, and he asked me to go look at houses with him that coming weekend. As he was doing back office work for a non-profit while still paying for his MBA, money was a little tight. It showed in the neighborhoods he took me around to see.

The temperature easily topped 110 the day we went to view properties. When it gets to that point, it feels like the sun is sitting just inches off your shoulders, threatening to blister your skin the minute you linger too long. At each new house we would hop out, run around to the side or back to look in, and dash back to the air-conditioned interior of the car. The homes were shabby, the yards little more than scraps of dirt, surrounded by rusted chain-link fences. Plastic children's toys broke the monotonous brown landscape. A pink fire truck, once red, cracked and unrideable, sat alongside a kiddie pool where wind-blown sediment had layered on the bottom. *I don't want my child growing up somewhere like this*. I checked my privilege when that thought crossed my mind; the children who lived here deserved just as pretty and safe an environment to grow up in, and just as bright of a future, as I wanted for mine.

And what about the people who loved this neighborhood, and had made happy homes for their families here? What did it mean to them that this neighborhood was considered to be gentrifying? Was this a good thing, signaling a new influx of money for the local establishments? Or would it simply drive up rents, making it more expensive for the people currently living here? What about these cases when doing what's "best" for our children is at odds with what's best for society as a whole?

Maybe it was the heat, or perhaps I was exhausted from the stress, but my brain felt foggy and I wanted to go home. The brightness of the sun and the constant hopping in and out of the AC amplified my irritation and made my shoulders come up around my ears, ready to wince at the slightest touch or offhand comment. I was on the verge of tears and I badly needed a nap. But the broker pushed on, wanting to look at a last handful of houses. I expressed my concerns about the safety of the neighborhood and the quality of the school district, particularly in a state with dismal public education to begin with. He countered that if I were willing to contribute my salary, we could move somewhere a lot nicer.

His voice became accusatory when he mentioned my salary; I was not being a team player. He took his eyes from the road and stared at me for an uncomfortable moment. I felt my back stiffen. I covered more than my share at home, and we both knew I had no desire to buy a place in Phoenix at all. I kept my response diplomatic; *I don't think it makes a lot of sense for us to buy right now. The last thing we need is more stress or change.* He kept his eyes fixed on the road as we merged onto the freeway. Speaking slowly, he began to lay out the state custody and child support laws that I would be bound to if I kept the child and it didn't work out between the two of us. As a father, he was entitled to every other weekend with a child, plus one weeknight per week. Since I was the primary breadwinner, I'd be paying him child support. It took a moment for my mind to catch up to his words. Beginning to grasp what he was implying, I felt numb. If we were to do this, I would be bound to him and he would do whatever he could to protect his rights. Understandable, if he'd wanted the child. But confusing, as he kept telling me he didn't. The mauve retaining walls of the freeway whizzed by, the decorative lizard and cacti murals nothing more than a blur of color. I sat mute the remainder of the ride home.

It didn't make sense to me. By taking me to look at houses, it seemed like he was ready to take this leap of faith together, but the next moment he was discussing the inevitable demise of our relationship. By now, a full week had passed since we'd found out and we'd been locked in a disaster of back and forths. I'd told him "I love you" for the first time and was met with silence. Then, later, when I told him I took a picture of myself in the mirror to start tracking any changes in my figure, he asked if I would send it to him too. I was confused and felt like I was living in a carnival house of mirrors, never sure what was real, or what might be right around the next corner. It all exhausted me. I couldn't help thinking, *maybe he's right, maybe we can't do this.* After another sleepless Sunday night, I set up an initial consultation at a "family planning clinic," with the possibility of a procedural appointment for the following weekend.

THE CLINIC WAS DOWNTOWN, NEAR to the broker's office and far from mine. It looked more like an office building than a medical complex, but the sign outside informed me that suites were filled with cardiologists, pain specialists and vascular disease physicians. Once inside, the decor was modern, all grey and white with a Keurig coffee machine in the corner and daytime TV playing too loudly on a screen next to the door.

The broker was late and I was well into filling out forms when he quietly sat down next to me, suit and tie on, wearing his best poker face. I was crying a steady drip of tears and doing my best to keep the papers dry. He saw my tears and asked me if I even wanted to be there. *Of course not. But do you want us to leave?* It was unkind, but it silenced him.

A friendly looking young woman in bright floral scrubs took us back to a room and spoke with us while taking my vitals. She gave us a run-down on what to expect and asked lots of questions about how I was doing so far, and if I understood what was involved in today's visit. The two of us nodded silently in response. She left the room so I could change into a gown for the physical exam. I looked around for a place to set my clothes and saw a small, grubby black plastic grocery basket on the floor. Once shiny, the basket was dull with scratches and had hair and bits of dust clinging to the bottom lattice. I balked at putting my clothes in. The broker offered to at least stuff my panties into his pocket to spare them so many imagined germs. I climbed up on the table and maneuvered my feet into the stirrups. It was awkward him being there; I'd never been in this position with a partner in the room before. Remembering why we were here, I felt tears stinging the backs of my eyes again. But now he was laughing. He leaned over me, kissed me on the forehead, and told me that having my panties in his pocket had turned him on. My brain nearly short-circuited: *Here?* Before I could think further, the doctor walked in, silencing all thoughts in my head.

She had short spiky hair and wore glasses. Her attitude was no-nonsense which I found surprising. I would have expected her to be softer and more sympathetic. The visit was tough but informative. We got to see a still dark circle on an ultrasound screen (I opted to look) and were explained the differences between a pill that would strip the lining of the uterus, resulting in something akin to a heavy period or early miscarriage; or a procedure which would mechanically remove the contents of the uterus. There was a 24-hour waiting period for either and if I wanted the procedure, I'd have to wait a few more days to be far enough along—six weeks.

At that point, the broker was asked to leave while I dressed and headed to a conference room for a private consultation with the doctor. Her manner softened immediately once we were alone. She offered me tissues and gave me ample time to respond to her questions. It was the opposite of the rushed doctor's appointments that seem to be the norm these days. She was a mother of four herself, she told me, and she asked how I imagined my future. *Not this*, I thought. I had always imagined my husband and I would go to sonogram appointments together, listen to the whoosh of a heartbeat, hold hands while we'd "ohh" and "ahh" over the little life we had created. Instead, my boyfriend was late for our appointment at the abortion clinic where he joked about getting a hard-on. My jaw tightened as I imagined years of biting my tongue in front of my child, rather than slander its other parent. I saw myself explaining to my child why rules were different at Daddy's house than at Mommy's house, while internally fighting the urge to scream. Or there was this Plan C, where we could opt out of parenthood altogether. The thought brought on another wave of tears.

In the car home our conversation circled back over familiar ground. I was a broken record, asking that he let me have the child and raise it on my own. He was unyielding. He did not want a child or the responsibility that came with it right now, but if I had it, he'd be involved. He reminded me again of his lunatic offer to freeze his sperm if I wanted to have his kid on my own one day.

Sometime during the days that followed, I broke up with him. *Once and for all*, I told myself. I knew I could be successful as a single parent, and I figured the sooner we made the break, the better. I was not deluding myself; I knew this would be a hard path, but I could clearly imagine my life being structured around a child. I recalled what the engineer said about the son he had half time: be solid, be stable, be *there* and your child will want to be with you. It was working for him, it could work for me—school activities, soccer coaching, weekend getaways, and always, always stability. Briefly, I felt my optimism bloom and my strength return to me. I pictured myself on the floor of an apartment, on an ordinary day together—me, and my daughter. Seated on the floor up against the wall, I'd raise her up, up over my head while she giggled with delight. I could imagine all the stress of single parenthood being swept away in my child's tinkling laughter.

But my sense of freedom was short-lived. He wouldn't let me back out that easily and his message was always the same; that we stay together regardless, but preferably without a child. He reassured me this one morning when we were on the phone, just after he'd been to the gym. I could hear his morning routine happening in the background—make eggs, do the dishes, iron a shirt for the day. He told me that someday we would be ready for a family—when we'd been together longer, when we were married, when we owned a home. *But the future won't change who we are*, I told him. *It's not about our circumstances, it's about us.* He proceeded to paint me a picture of *his* promised land: him arriving home from work and trying to solve the puzzle of how to fit

41

both me and a child in his arms at the same time. The broker couldn't get past the current hardships we felt like we were facing: when would he have the chance to start his own business, where would we live, who would be the primary caregiver? I wasn't convinced by his argument that now was the wrong time to have a child, but he did convince me to at least have dinner with him that evening to check in. After dinner I agreed to try again. I felt so weak, so uncertain, but I just didn't want to be alone.

The breakup and subsequent reconciliation had left me at a low emotional ebb. I was angry with myself for not having the strength to *get this nightmare over with*. How could I ever co-parent with this person? Recalling the instructions from the woman at the clinic, I knew my state-mandated 24-hour waiting period was over and I scheduled a procedural appointment for that coming Saturday. Even if I couldn't leave this relationship that day, at least I didn't have to be tied to him forever.

I HARDLY SLEPT THE NIGHT before I was due to go in. A ball of nerves in the morning, breakfast was not an option as I moved from room to room in his house, as if my pacing might help me escape the truth of where we were headed in just a few hours' time. He wasn't in much better shape himself. He was quiet and a little sharp with me, a tough combination in my anxious, overwrought state. He'd spoken to me once already about my crying all the time. By this point I was pretty unable to get a handle on it, though I tried, biting the side of my tongue hard as the tears threatened to overwhelm me.

And then I stopped. I stopped moving, stopped trying not to cry, stopped trying to make the situation anything it wasn't. I sat, balanced on the edge of the couch, face in my hands as I realized I just couldn't do this. Chloe walked over and rested her face on the couch next to me, gazing up at me with her soulful brown eyes, and let out a huge sigh, the way dogs do. I choked my way through an unintelligible sentence to the broker. He came over and sat with me and asked me to repeat myself. *I can't do this.* He was quiet for a moment, gathering his thoughts. Then he asked if I wanted to go to Sedona instead.

You know when somebody says something so out of left field that it catches you totally off guard? This was one of those moments. *Sedona?* Sedona. To get away for the weekend. To set all of this aside, not think about it, and just enjoy ourselves. *Us, like we used to be.* I laughed for the first time in what felt like forever. *Tough decision.* Every time it felt like all hope was lost, the wind changed direction again.

PHOENICIANS LOVE TO ESCAPE TO Sedona in the summers to get away from the heat of the valley. We escaped there to get away from the heat of our relationship. It offered us a perfect break from reality—we were out of the 100-degree heat, no talk about the pregnancy. Instead we spent our time playing with Chloe in Oak Creek, the clear water tickling her feet, the boulders in the creek smooth and difficult for her claws to get a grip on. She splashed hilariously through the water every time she fell off. We stayed at a small hotel in town with dark purple carpet and Hopi Kachina dolls in the lobby. We went for a hearty, if not romantic, dinner, and spent the evening playing Yahtzee. He won every game. Things were a little awkward between us, but it was clear we were both making an effort, and we did at least snuggle on those nights away from home.

Sunday morning arrived too soon. We had breakfast and went out for one last hike. We took a selfie, and it's the only picture I have of the two of us from when I was pregnant. The sun was blinding, and our eyes are hidden by sunglasses. A stand of Arizona Cypress and the famous Sedona Red Rocks were our backdrop, the rugged desolation of the desert somehow befitting the situation. Our smiles look flat to me.

On our way back into town, we stopped at a locally renowned cafe, just off the I-17. I had never been, and the broker wanted to introduce me to their famous fruit pies. It was also a nice break from the car for

Chloe, and I took her to find some water and look for a good place to sit while he ordered. The cottonwoods were huge and swayed in the warm wind, the traffic from the highway quieter than I expected. The broker arrived with the pies; peach for me, cherry for him. We sat in companionable silence in the grass. I mostly picked at the food on my plate, my mind leaping ahead to what awaited us back in real life.

You look sad, he commented. I've never been able to conceal my emotions. I looked up at the sky—bright blue with super puffy clouds. Sometimes looking at the sky, remembering the enormity of the universe helps me gain some perspective. How small my problems might seem to others. How impossibly huge they seemed to me. I glanced at him, *did the weekend change anything for you?* As if a 48-hour escape from our problems could somehow prove that we might make it as a family. I knew the answer before I asked the question, but still I hoped. In my heart I knew he wanted to be a father one day. *Would he take the leap today?* He shook his head.

BACK HOME, NOW MORE THAN two weeks since we'd found out, my exhaustion returned and I felt myself backed into a corner. If we were going to terminate the pregnancy, that window was closing quickly for me, adding even more pressure. I read somewhere that a woman wants an abortion like an animal in a trap wants to chew its own leg off. I couldn't imagine a better metaphor for how I felt. Opting for an abortion is a miserable choice. But bringing a child into this toxic relationship and being bound to the broker for life seemed the greater of the two evils.

Looking back now, from a place where I believe I would have chosen a different road, I wonder: *Why, if I have a history of making really good decisions, was I having such a hard time with this?* I found an explanation in *Awakening the Brain* by Charlotte A. Tomaino—a nun turned neuropsychologist—that helped me understand. "The ability to think broadly, creatively, and intelligently is absent when the sympathetic

nervous system takes over... it literally makes you stupid. After experiencing such an arousal state, people often ask themselves, 'What
was I thinking?' The answer is that you weren't thinking, because
you couldn't." Our sympathetic nervous system is what triggers the
fight-or-flight response in our bodies. What Dr. Tomaino is getting at
is the idea that we can't get into problem-solving mode when we're
panicking. Say, when you find out your boyfriend is a porn addict and
discover that you're pregnant with his child *on the same day.*

Dr. Tomaino goes on to explain that during periods of extended
stress—when things aren't going well and your physical and emotional needs aren't being met—it doesn't take much to switch into a state
of hyperarousal (fight-or-flight). This helped to explain the constant
push and pull I was feeling. I was low on sleep, not eating well, and
under constant emotional stress. Add in the mounting time pressure,
and what few moments of clarity I had always seemed to dissipate
into confusion and anxiety.

There would be one more almost-procedure at the clinic on my
path to abortion. We'd finally agreed that we weren't ready to be parents together, but on the day of the appointment I was a confused
wreck once again. I cried openly in the office, and the staff kept asking me if I was really sure—clearly made uneasy by my outpouring of
emotion. I'd made it to the point where I had the gown on to have the
procedure, when the broker asked one last time if I was sure. I looked
him in the eyes, *No.* For as much as I didn't want to be a parent, I didn't
want to have an abortion more. The broker pulled me off the table and
brought me my clothes. We were both a little wobbly and near tears.
In the lobby on our way out the door, the spiky haired doctor popped
her head into the waiting area and asked us to send along a birth an-
nouncement, *we love getting those.* She gave me a quick hug and waved to
the broker. We assured her we would and left the clinic hand in hand.

After walking out of the clinic, we went back to the house, now
ours since I had signed away the lease on my apartment. We were go-

ing to grab a quick bite before heading back into work, when I heard him in the kitchen on FaceTime with his mom and sister. He called me over to him, and once I was in the picture, he said "oops." None of us understood what was happening, myself included, until he explained that we'd had an "oops" and now I was part of the family. I smiled awkwardly and looked down at my feet. His mom and sister were wonderful and supportive and offered any help we'd need, be it during the pregnancy or after the child was born. When we hung up the phone I asked him to explain himself—we had never discussed telling our parents. *If we cancelled that appointment I guess we're keeping it.* I was too tired to be mad at him, but I was unhappy that he'd told his family. Yes, we'd walked out of the clinic, but I still wanted the back door left open. Now that he'd told them, I felt even more trapped.

I had been wanting to tell my own mother the whole time I'd been pregnant, but had held off both because it was early, and because we were considering terminating the pregnancy. But now that his family knew, I asked if he would join me in telling my mom that afternoon at her house.

We met at her place after work, and once we'd all said our hellos, I told her. This wasn't how I saw this conversation going in my life, telling my mom I was pregnant when I'd been at an abortion clinic earlier in the day, but here I was. Tired, a little confused, but so happy to tell my mom in person. She lit up. She put her hands up to her face and then back down, she turned around, unable to digest what we'd said and the joy it brought her. She'd been waiting years for this moment. My half-brother's children are grown, and since my brother is a priest, I'm the only child who will bear her grandchildren. Seeing the elation on her face was at once the most wonderful and the most terrifying thing. I was so happy to see her wish to be a grandmother fulfilled, and so frightened for my own future in that moment.

If anything, rather than bring an end to the back and forth between us, this seeming stake in the ground only amplified our fighting over the coming days. We still hadn't made a conscious decision to have a child together—not when we had unprotected sex, and not when we left the abortion clinic that day. If anything, our fate was the product of indecision, the winds of fortune steering our increasingly shaky ship.

Three weeks to the day from when the test came back with those two pink, life-changing lines, we had lunch at our favorite local restaurant. It had a patio overlooking the Arizona Canal, and was an easy bike ride from our house. Neither of us was interested in the hubbub and congeniality of the patio and so we sat inside for a change, sheltered and out of view. We were both solemn, and he confessed that he'd spent the previous week hoping for a text from me saying that I had gone in alone and taken the pills. *It would give me a new lease on life*, he said. As if he was staring down the barrel of a gun with this pregnancy. If we didn't have a child, it would give him the opportunity to do all the things he'd been putting off. I looked around the room at the hipster, microbrewery decor. Antique bike parts on the walls, road signs, and unfinished wood. The place suddenly seemed chintzy and worn to me. As useless as it was, for just one moment I wished it were his body that carried this child, not mine—that way the decision wouldn't be mine to make. Had it been up to him, there would not have been this back and forth. He didn't want it. He would have had the procedure as quickly as possible. I picked at my salad, the vibrantly colored vegetables somehow flat to me. I was exhausted. Spent. I couldn't see a way to have the child as a single mom and wouldn't have this child with the broker. I didn't know it at the time, but this was the last meal we'd share together as future parents.

THE FOLLOWING MORNING, I FOUND my resolve and called the clinic to make what would be my final appointment. I went alone, the staff at this point recognizing who I was. The spiky haired doctor and a floral scrub clad PA were in the room with me when I took the pill. I was in my work clothes—business casual—having come down there on yet another long lunch. The room was particularly cold and the air conditioning cut through my flimsy blouse. My heart rate was sky-high and my hands were shaking and clammy. I was terrified. If the doctor or PA noticed, they said nothing. They handed the pill to me in a small, white paper cup. The pill was nondescript and didn't look as though it could take a life—it looked more like a low dose aspirin. I swallowed it the moment the doctor let go of the cup, before any more indecision could set in. *Let's get this nightmare over with.* They gave me painkillers and a small Manila envelope with five additional pills in it. I was instructed to put them in my cheeks after 24 hours had passed.

It was lunchtime when I arrived home and called the broker. He was surprised by the news. The silence on the phone was thick; I could hear him digesting what I had just told him. *Do you need me to come home?* I was okay, I told him, but I let him know that he could take the following afternoon off if he wanted to sit with me when I took the final set of pills. He didn't ask any more questions.

All day I had kept a stiff upper lip. Finally alone, I allowed myself to fall apart. I took a painkiller, pulled the drapes in the bedroom, and went to bed sobbing.

THE ABORTION ITSELF WAS UNEVENTFUL. From what I have heard from the four friends who have recounted their miscarriages to me, it went like that. To me, it seemed like the worst period I've ever had.

I had to wait 24 to 48 hours after I took the first pill to take the second set. I had the world's most anxious day and night, unable to focus, eat, or sleep.

As soon as the 24-hour mark rolled around I took the second set of pills. There were five of them and instead of swallowing them, the instructions said to tuck them into my cheeks, like a chipmunk. As soon as that was done, I panicked and realized I should take Chloe out one more time before we settled in to wait. I only had her outside for about five minutes but was so nervous for what might happen that my kneecaps bobbed up and down uncontrollably every time she stopped to sniff something. We got right back to the house and I spent the afternoon expecting the bleeding to start any moment, but nothing came. I picked at my dinner with the broker—my appetite was still lacking—and went to bed early, again anticipating that I would wake up to the bleeding.

Morning came, still nothing. I worried that the pills hadn't worked and called the clinic. They told me I was still within the range of normal, and that I should call again the next morning if there were no changes. I walked Chloe, tried to focus on some work, and called my mom who offered to come spend time with me. I assured her I was okay.

It wasn't until after lunch that the cramps finally started, mild at first but progressing to be more intense than normal. I had a heating pad, took some ibuprofen, and settled into the couch. When the bleeding started it was a lot. I typically have light and short periods, so this amount of blood was new to me. There was also tissue, and with every trip to the bathroom I checked to see if I could see a fetus—by seven and a half weeks I was told it would be nearly the size of a blueberry. I never saw anything, and wondered what I would do if I did. The reality that whatever that life was, was ending in our sewage system was a difficult thought to bear. I was relieved I never saw anything more distinct than some clots of blood.

The broker came home from work early that day at my request. He sat with me on the couch, and we watched *Band of Brothers*. I am a grade-A bibliophile, a bookworm in every sense of the word. For each event in my life, I can remember the book I was reading at the time. But that day, words on a page were too difficult for me to hold onto. Knowing my fondness for history, and in particular WWII history, his recommendation for the show was spot on. My paternal grandfather served in the European theater in WWII, earning a purple heart for shots taken to his knees, and a Bronze Star for his heroic service in a key battle. I could imagine my grandfather in that story, his love of Patton, his descriptions of the European countryside during the war—the damage taken to the buildings—always looking forward to a new ration of coffee or cigarettes. It made me feel connected to him at a moment when I was losing a future piece of my family.

The cramping ebbed and flowed throughout the afternoon, but it seemed like the whole thing was done by the time we went to bed. I didn't sleep soundly, but was less anxious knowing the worst was over. The following day I was able to go back to work, and I went to my mom's house the next night for a hug and a good cry. I decided to stay the night, and woke at three in the morning with the worst cramps I experienced through the entire abortion. I assume a small piece of matter was still in my uterus and that my body was working hard to clear it. In the morning there was a little more blood, a little more tissue, and that truly was the end.

I went to the doctor later that week for a check-up. I received a clean bill of health, and they even saw multiple late-stage follicles forming: a sign of the next set of eggs getting ready to be released. The spiky haired doctor who saw me through the whole journey told me it was over, I was healthy, and wished me the best. I tried to express my gratitude for what she did for my life, but no words felt sufficient.

I drove myself home, relieved.

three

Just over a year after the abortion, I was in a women's locker room getting ready for work after a master's swim practice. The pool is by the waterfront and so the locker room always smells faintly of the sea. The facility was constructed back in 1937, with a history (mostly of being burned down and rebuilt) that dates back to the 1870s. The locker room itself has a distinctly 1970s feel to it, with mustard yellow tiles and well-worn wooden benches. The younger team also swims at that pool, and this morning I was sharing the locker room with a gaggle of high school girls who'd just wrapped up their workout as well. They chatted away next to me, alternately discussing boys at their school and fiercely debating whether or not Korea was an island. Eventually their conversation turned to a recent writing assignment: an argumentative essay for or against abortion.

To a woman, they sang the same tune, *I'm pro-choice, but I'd never have one myself.* Their voices had dropped and you could tell they took the topic seriously. Although they said they were pro-choice and supported other women's right to choose, when it came to the idea of them having an abortion themselves, they almost seemed more pro-life. *I could never live with myself if I did that*, one of them said.

This came as no surprise to me. For the first 34 or so years of my life, when I thought of abortion at all, that was my line. Like these young women, I grew up in an upper-middle class household in various affluent towns, with little to worry about beyond how conservatively my mom dressed me compared to my friends (I eventually won the spaghetti strap war, but it took some convincing). In lieu of a discussion about sex, my parents gave me a flimsy pink booklet to read. Faceless bubble diagrams of men and women accompanied the clinical terms describing the act. I remember my mom giving me the booklet on the drive home from school one day. I was captive in the car and had nowhere to hide my embarrassment. I stuffed it in my book bag to be read later, away from the prying eyes of my parents. Even alone in my bedroom I was flustered reading the parts detailing sex, though I was fascinated by the diagrams of our reproductive organs. It was the first time I remember wondering about the "spark" of life. Eventually my parents asked if I had read the book. I said I had, and the sex talk ended there. When the conversation turned to dating and pregnancy I was told that I was too young to date, and that babies were for marriage.

The topic of abortion never came up during this conversation. It also wasn't covered in our health classes at my school. I later found out that was thanks to the Adolescent Family Life Act of 1981. The primary goal of the so-called Chastity Act was to "prevent premarital teen pregnancy" by establishing "'family-centered' programs" to "promote chastity and self-discipline.'" This act was upheld in the Supreme Court in 1988 and again in 1991. To her credit, my high school health teacher, an eccentric older woman with silver hair, never cited abortion as murder, instead she opted to never mention it. Since neither my parents nor my educators ever brought it up, it was no surprise that I didn't consider abortion when I was learning about sex. When I did think of it, it fell into the realm of "other." In my mind I saw someone unkempt; maybe she did drugs and had unsafe sex with too many men. Perhaps she had dealt with STDs, was in and out of jobs and debt, and lived in subsidized housing. Basically, she was all the things my family was not. Now, I wonder about my younger self— where did that stereotype come from? I never stopped to consider why any woman would find herself in the above position, or the life of oppression or trauma that had led her there. Why would any of these external circumstances make her a bad person?

All I knew then was that abortion was not something that happened to families "like mine." At church once, friends of my parents joked that their newborn baby was a "surprise," and they glowed with joy, expressing how *lucky* they were to have made that mistake. At that age, it never crossed my mind that maybe these couples had considered abortion, but decided to keep the pregnancy instead. Because these women were all pro-choice, *but they'd never have an abortion themselves.*

AFTER I TOOK THE PILLS that would end my pregnancy, I went silent. My brother had recently joined a religious order, my mother was busy with daily trips to my father's long-term care facility where she was his consummate advocate and loving wife, and my boyfriend was tired of my tears. I felt adrift, unsure, and ultimately alone. In the quiet evening hours when the broker was working late I'd be alone at "our" place, but could never quite comfort myself there. In some intuitive move of self-preservation I refused to move my things in with me, instead I'd just packed a suitcase and lived out of that. To escape the dark furniture imbued with his smell, I would take Chloe for long walks, looking at my decision from another angle, and another again.

I wasn't sure where my beliefs fell on the spectrum of what defined "a life," and although I didn't feel like a murderer, I knew I had stopped *something* in its tracks. *I'm a monster. No one knows how bad I really am.* I still spoke with Laura from time to time, and while she was compassionate and supportive, her situation had been so different from mine that I could easily justify her actions where I could only condemn myself. She was young when she got pregnant and therefore didn't know better. I, on the other hand, had 20 years of menstrual cycles behind me and should have known how my body worked by now.

The broker didn't seem to have such concerns, or if he did, he didn't voice them with me. Somehow the abortion seemed to make our relationship take a turn for the better. We had weathered this storm—imperfectly, but together—and it seemed like maybe this was the trial that would unite us as a couple. *What doesn't kill us makes us stronger.* Not to mention, I had become fixated on "making it work." Part of me reasoned that if we could still get married and have kids *one day*, somehow it would make the thing I did less awful, not in vain. I felt like I had flunked a test of my morality, like I had failed my child, and that by having an abortion I had alienated myself from the hallowed land of motherhood. If together we could learn something from that experience and elevate our lives to a higher plane where children did make sense, then that child's life would have meaning.

Alone with my thoughts, I did what any rational person would do—turned to the internet to validate my hypothesis. It turns out plenty of couples had experienced exactly this scenario. A young woman on her way to becoming a PA had fallen pregnant but wanted to finish school first. After the abortion and getting her degree, she and her then boyfriend eventually married and had the family they wanted. Another couple was just starting out, money incredibly tight. Once they were closer to their 30s, they had their children and built a successful business alongside their family. Maybe this would be our path too? The broker didn't have many opinions when I raised the topic with him. He felt as though he'd dodged a bullet, and seemed to be staying true to his word about the abortion having given him a new lease on life; he began to do his due diligence on opening his own firm.

Days and weeks went by and we were steady, if not good: the broker compartmentalizing and disappearing into work, while I continued to try to find stories like my own. The initial panic of finding out I was pregnant and the turmoil of making the decision having passed, I was markedly less tense. I could feel the letdown in my body—my shoulders weren't up around my ears all the time and I felt like I could breathe easily again. I still wasn't sharing my story with any of my friends because I didn't want anyone to see me how I had secretly come to see myself: a woman who'd had an abortion. How could they remain friends with me if they knew? Some of my more liberal girlfriends, sure, they'd applaud me for *doing what was best for me*, but I couldn't kick the sense that I had become a marked woman.

I didn't realize how much I was internalizing everything and eventually the broker and I fell back into our old patterns. We'd argue when we were together—I wanted to talk about what we'd been through, he just wanted to move on. His non-responses to my questions left me stinging. We took a quick trip to California in an effort to keep things together. On the drive, we had the weirdest argument about him not wanting the PIN to unlock my phone. Only months later would I realize this was because he didn't want to have to share access to his phone with me. Later in that trip, as we were walking back to a parking garage from some time on the beach, he stonewalled me for having spent too much time swimming the buoy line in the ocean one morning, and leaving him alone on the blanket.

The final morning of our trip I woke up in a blind panic, confused about where I was. My heart was racing, and I was covered in a clammy sweat. A strange comforter was tangled around my legs, the bed seemed to be facing the wrong way, and the curtains were letting light in strangely. *That's right, I'm in California.* What had me so panicked? Was it a nightmare? I got up to drink a glass of water and sat on the couch in the room watching the broker sleep in the dim light, his breath deep and even. The covers were around his waist and his back was exposed. His shoulders were broad and ropy from all the climbing and he had perfectly smooth skin. He truly was a handsome man. After a moment of stillness, I could finally place my anxiety: *what if I get pregnant again?* I was on birth control again, and we were both so spooked about getting pregnant that we were using condoms too. It seemed unlikely, but it was on my mind.

After that realization, my obsession with making things work between us shifted. I had enough headspace to recognize that our relationship was living at the intersection of "bad" and "not changing." The question of whether or not to leave him created a constant battleground in my head. I'd chase thoughts in zigzagging circles: *I don't want to be with him. But am I really ready to be alone? I don't trust him. But I should stay until I'm absolutely certain.* I wanted out, but was afraid of how much it was going to hurt, and I was even more afraid that the pain of leaving him would just keep me coming back. It was exactly these mental gymnastics that kept me in the relationship in the first place, before I was even pregnant. Exhausted by my own thoughts, I always landed back in the same place: *fuck, this is my life. And I can't escape.*

To counter my feelings of paralysis, I started writing lists of all the things I *could* do: I could eat a healthy diet, I could run and swim, I could spend time with my most uplifting friends, I could see a therapist (I found two—the one I liked rarely had availability, so I needed a second as a backup—plus a life coach), I could get acupuncture to calm my nerves. Anything that would shift my energy in a positive direction seemed like a worthwhile pursuit. And while my thoughts and feelings about what I had done didn't change overnight, my mind began to open.

My life coach, Laila, whom I still see today, related my thoughts to teeth: we weren't trying to pull them out, we just wanted to wiggle them. Her point being that not every passing thought was rooted in the capital-T truth, that thoughts were just stories, and that maybe those stories could be re-written with alternate narratives. The stories we tell ourselves shape the way we view our world. If the stories we have on repeat in our heads have us playing the role of compassionate, kind, caring people, then we'll view ourselves with those attributes in situations throughout our lives. Alternatively, and sadly more often, our narratives are filled with criticism, shame, and judgment—a lens through which we'd never see our close friends. The longer we have told ourselves these stories, the deeper their roots are in our psyches.

This is why Laila was starting with small thoughts.

We worked together over the phone and I often took calls before or after my workday, but still at my office building—it's where I had the most privacy. I liked to sit in one of the conference rooms that faced east over the desert. Our building was mostly glass and concrete and we had floor to ceiling windows, with wall-to-wall grey carpeting and furniture. The designers were clearly going for "modern," but they kind of overshot and landed in the neighborhood of "bleak and barren." One evening on the phone, she asked if I'd ever considered that I might have miscarried had I not had an abortion. The sun was lowering and the sky was pastel blue—it wouldn't be one of Arizona's iconic blazing sunsets that evening. Impossible, I told her. I was healthy and came from a fertile family. *Just go with this*, she implored. I thought about it. I had ended the pregnancy before the eight-week mark; just recently a good friend had just had her second miscarriage immediately on the other side of that milestone. *A possibility, I guess*. She explained to me her point: there was no way for us to know what could have happened had I kept the pregnancy. There were an infinite number of outcomes that in our wildest dreams we couldn't imagine. What if one of those outcomes had been horrible? What if I had spared a child all that suffering? If I could consider this other potential outcome, then perhaps my most tried-and-true story could also be seen in another light: *maybe I'm not a monster after all.*

ONCE I FOUND MY FOOTING with the idea that I was a good, moral person after all, I began to tell my story to friends I trusted. It was terrifying—and still is—but I wanted to lessen the burden on myself and seek support on my journey. Some of my friends I spoke to on the phone, with others it was hikes, brunches, and dinners. The conversations were never done in one sitting. I sought out friends with a balanced mindset. Abortion so frequently falls into the landscape of being either sacred or profane. I wanted to talk to women who, like me, saw how pregnancy could be both a miracle and a physical event; that a fetus could be a child but was currently a grouping of cells, and that abortion could be wrong, but could also be very right—depending on the circumstances. Those friends were easy to find: grounded and no-nonsense, while maintaining their compassion and kindness.

I expected my friends to be supportive, and I hoped they'd also be open-minded. What I didn't expect to learn was how many of the women I knew had also had an abortion, or a miscarriage, or any number of fertility issues. What I discovered was that human reproductive issues are universal. And yet the shame we feel around these topics is so overwhelming, we'll do just about anything to conceal the reality of our experiences. Amelia Bonow, of the group Shout Your Abortion, says, "Plenty of people still believe that on some level—if you are a good woman—abortion is a choice which should be accompanied by some level of sadness, shame, or regret." The vestige of this sentiment rings out in my good girl expression: *I'm pro-choice, but I'd never have one myself.*

I've come to believe that this line is doing us—women, society—a disservice. It keeps abortion in the realm of "other" and validates the trope that only "bad girls" have them. When I was younger, around the age of the young women I overheard in the locker room, I didn't have the foresight to understand how that statement would turn its back on me when I found myself pregnant. To maintain my good girl status, I'd either have to keep the child, or keep my abortion secret. In the introduction of *Choice Words*, an anthology of abortion stories, feminist poet Annie Finch says that the stories in the book "describe the tragic emotional and physical toll of cultural, political, and religious attempts to force us to have children, to force us to have abortions, or to surround our reproductive choices with shame, silence, and isolation." By the time abortion entered my consciousness, I had been indoctrinated by the collective shame around it, and knew it was something good girls didn't do. Until I did it myself. Opening up about my choice—talking to friends, reading other women's abortion accounts, and finally viewing my choice without judgment—allowed me to come to realize that the shame I carried was less about me and more about society.

Many of the women I spoke with hadn't told anyone what they'd been through. Not their mothers, daughters, sisters, husbands, cousins or friends. Many of them still felt guilt and other strong negative emotions. For some it had been years; for others, decades. What kind of damage is done to the human psyche when a person keeps hold of a secret with this level of emotional charge for two years, or 10, or 50? How can we expect it to be different for future generations of women if we can't find a way to speak our truths?

In the 1960s the Women's Liberation Movement did just this. In her book, *Birth Strike*, Jenny Brown explains that "collectively examining our experiences on abortion and birth control was necessary to get us the reforms we have now, and it will be at the heart of any advances we make in the future." My conversations with my friends were hardly on the scale of those sparked by Gloria Steinem when she launched *Ms* magazine in 1972, featuring the names of 53 women who admitted to having abortions and sparking a national debate on the issue. But to me they felt like a start. Talking to these women brought me a sense of relief, and I could only imagine they felt the same, because many wanted to continue these conversations.

As I learned about the circumstances of other women's abortions, I discovered it was easy for me to grant them a pass in terms of their responsibility: this friend was so young, this other friend never wanted kids and was on birth control, and another had medical issues that should have prevented this from happening. But not me. At the time, my lens was laser-focused on the issue of getting pregnant. As though, if getting pregnant weren't your fault, then you got a pass for having an abortion. A young woman might not understand the sheer strength of her fertility, a woman on birth control was doing her best.

But me, I had knowingly had unprotected sex. *How could I allow something like this to happen?*

As I was working through all of these feelings, I had dinner with my friend Julie, who I'd known for nearly two decades. She's about 15 years older than me and has two kids: one in high school, one in college. She is Christian, generally conservative, and has always been real with me. When I was struggling with depression, she shared her own story of depression. When things weren't going swimmingly with the direction of my life, she was there to remind me: I was young, this was normal.

The night we met for dinner, she was in the middle of an exceptionally ugly divorce. We were at her new rental house, and I was standing at the counter chopping vegetables for a Greek salad I was making. Her place was still quite empty since she'd just moved in. Her kitchen counter had no stools, so she sat at a hand-me-down oak table. Our line of sight wasn't always clear because of the counter height and that gave us a good laugh. As we spoke, I began to share some of the more gnarly details of my relationship with the broker but was afraid to mention the abortion. I looked down and realized that my hands had begun to shake with adrenaline. I knew I was going to tell her, but I had an overwhelming fear that she'd never speak to me again. I made myself set down the knife and turned to tell her that at some point during my relationship, I found out I was pregnant. The rest of the sentence stuck in my throat and I had to swallow a couple of times before I could continue. I looked down, more ashamed than I had been when telling anyone else. *And I had an abortion.* I slapped my hands over my face as my breath came in gasps. I stood rooted to the spot, trying not to cry. She put her arms around me, and I felt her whisper through my hair: *I've had one too.*

The ground fell out from underneath me. It seemed as though I was tipping sideways and the only thing holding me up was her hug. Julie was *not that kind of a woman*. Even today, more than a year after that conversation, I continue to have a hard time reconciling her "good girl" appearance with the fact she had an abortion. And yet, she did.

Her circumstances were different from mine. She had been put into a medical menopause because of health issues she was facing at the time. Again, I found myself giving her a pass on having an abortion—after all, she was doing the right things, it wasn't her fault. In our discussion I realized that she didn't view how I got pregnant as something to be ashamed of, nor did she feel like the circumstances of her pregnancy gave her a "pass" on having an abortion—it was not a hard choice for her to make, but she still felt badly that it had to happen.

We debriefed on this conversation several months later, and it almost felt like we were a new couple discussing our first kiss: *wait, so you felt this way all along?* Julie was abashed that I was afraid to tell her, as though my hesitation showed her to be a person who came off as judgmental. I felt just the opposite. I had projected my own self-judgment onto her, assuming she would view me as reckless and irresponsible for getting pregnant, and amoral and even more irresponsible for deciding to terminate my pregnancy.

As I listened to story after story like this from the women in my life, I began to wonder how different my feelings about my own situation would have been if abortion were something we spoke about freely. Like the *fact of life* that it currently is. Kristen Ghodsee, an accomplished ethnographer and gender studies researcher, wrote an essay detailing the casual attitudes towards abortion that women in "former communist countries" have. Women in these nations have relied on abortion as a primary form of birth control since the 1950s. A woman she met for dinner one evening mentioned she was late because she'd had an abortion that morning. Ghodsee was shocked with the ease with which she spoke about her abortion and writes: "I'd spent almost all of my adult life on hormonal birth control to avoid getting pregnant because I was terrified of both having an unwanted child and of having an abortion. In my mind abortion meant trauma, regret, and emotional *sturm und drang.* In the US, abortion was a big deal. People killed over it. Could it really be that in Bulgaria it was just something you did on the way to the post office?" I can't see the US becoming that progressive about abortion any time soon. However, if we as a society were more willing to be open about the fact that *this happens*, could we all be spared the shame and mental anguish that accompanies abortion? Which is not to say I would not have felt grief about my choice in the same way that I have sadness about many of the roads not taken in my life. But maybe I could have faced this decision without staring down a lifetime sentence of societal shame that left me questioning *who I even am.*

Although every woman's story is different, just like every woman's life and background is different, learning the real story about someone else's experience always reflects back to us pieces and parts of ourselves. The conversations I've had with friends like Julie who have been through this same thing have been as healing as the therapy I invested in to help myself make sense of it all; that is the power of vulnerably sharing our stories. In the introduction of her book, *You're the Only One I've Told*, Meera Shah, a doctor who specializes in sexual and reproductive health, says, "the simple act of sharing stories is one of the most effective ways to influence, teach, and inspire change. Storytelling creates emotional connections between people ... Even if an individual can't identify with another's exact experience, there is usually some component of the story, even as small as the fleeting, universal emotions of fear or happiness, that can be shared or appreciated."

Telling our stories also gives a voice to our bodies, helping us to re-familiarize ourselves with our inner emotional or physical landscape after a major life event. Learning about other people's experiences can open our perspectives on what is "normal," much like when I found out about how abortion was handled in former communist countries. And more than anything else, sharing with our trusted friends helps us feel whole within our own community.

In his landmark book on trauma, *The Body Keeps the Score*, Bessel Van Der Kolk explains, "Study after study shows that having a good support network constitutes the single most powerful protection against being traumatized." The therapeutic potential of solidarity and forgiveness is accessible to everyone and can begin by opening up to a trusted friend, or even with the simple act of sharing a book. It's the basis of talk therapy: sharing our story with a trusted other gives us the ability to change our perspectives and move forward with our lives.

I BEGAN THERAPY ABOUT SIX weeks after the abortion and following another failed attempt at leaving the broker. There was no event that made me leave that particular day, I just finally felt ready, felt strong enough. Evidently that wasn't the case. In my initial session with one of the therapists I found, Noah, he asked what my life would look like if I could leave his office that day with everything resolved. *I'd be single, and out of Arizona.* Leaving the broker was my highest priority, in part because I was so fearful of becoming pregnant again, even though I was back on birth control and we were being extra cautious. In addition to that, I wanted to sort through some of the more complex emotions I was feeling about the abortion.

Therapy wasn't fun at this juncture, it reminded me of a bad day running: you're at the limit of a sustainable pace and yet when you look at your watch, you're nowhere near where you want to be—all that effort, so little to show. My appointments were in the morning before work, and on arriving at my office afterwards I'd park in a dark corner of our underground garage and sit, numb and blank, staring at the grey concrete wall, allowing stillness to permeate me. Slowly, life would come back into my limbs, thoughts into my head, and color back into the world in front of me. During the sessions, Noah's line of questioning often brought up hot emotions like fear and anger. After those emotions had burned through my body, the balance of the day

I felt anesthetized or deflated. Those days acted as a momentary reprieve from the dumpster fire that was my life.

In one memorable appointment, Noah and I discussed two of my recent dreams. In the first, I caught the broker in bed with another woman, and he looked at me and laughed at my dawning realization of what was happening. In the second, I was galloping through a city on a horse I rode in my teens and twenties. Tonic was tall and strong, grey in color—closer to white in his later years—the type of horse who would make calm decisions on a cross-country course regardless of my level of nerves. In my dream, I was riding bareback through the fog in a city that looked much like historical London. The streets were cobbled and lined with gas lamps. I couldn't see the uneven surface below the fog and that scared me, but I held fast to his mane and gave over completely to his direction; I knew I would be unable to find my own way, and that I could trust his instincts.

Noah barely spoke about the first dream—the one where the broker was cheating on me. It seemed self-explanatory to him. It was the second dream he wanted to talk about. He believed it was showing me that I could trust my intuition, that my higher-level consciousness could navigate for me when I felt I could not take the next step forward myself. He told me to lean into that sense, to stop ignoring all the red flags that I had so clearly identified. Like the dog in the meme, my house was on fire but I was still sipping my coffee telling anyone who'd listen: *everything's fine.*

In the end, the dream about the broker cheating on me proved to be a powerful portent, intruding on my thoughts day after day. My life at this point reminded me of so many stories of alcoholics trying to quit drinking; they'll do anything to quit drinking ... except quit drinking. Here I was going to all kinds of therapy, setting intentions, saying affirmations. I had a dropper of flower essences for strength for heaven's sake, but I still hadn't done the one thing that would ultimately get me out of my relationship: leave.

One morning, shortly after Christmas, the broker was out of the house walking Chloe when I decided to check his phone. He had told me his PIN a couple of times, and with *great* effort I'd finally remembered it. Before that day, I had only looked one time to see what apps he had installed. I chose not to look more often because I wanted to trust him. Something inside me that winter day told me to trust myself more. I wanted to see his texts, and decided I was only going to look at the first page. No scrolling. When I opened his messages I immediately saw a woman's name I didn't recognize, Jen Young. A picture next to her name showed her: gaze upward into the camera, round cheeks and long brown hair tumbling over her shoulders. Sultry. I opened the thread, *More naked time? More naked time?* My brain couldn't catch up with what I was reading. I closed the phone without scrolling and set it down on the black granite countertop. I felt odd, like I was falling, but maybe sideways. My mind immediately jumped in with rapid-fire thoughts: this would be another fight; he would defend his right to have "open" conversations with his female friends even though I found it inappropriate. *You're so uptight,* was his go-to defense. I turned around, eyes fixed on the white tile floor, and started to walk away from the phone, frustrated.

Then something inside me roared. From the depths of my being, I felt electricity surge out of the top of my head, thoughts gone, my brain blown out with white noise. My body moved of its own accord back to the phone, as though I was on the horse from my dream. I entered the PIN, opened the thread and scrolled up. Directions to our house. Explicit details of what they had done. *That motherfucker.*

It was an expensive price to pay, and not an experience I want to go through again, but I knew it was finally over. I began to pack that day before he was back from his walk. My one silver suitcase and a laundry basket of random kitchen appliances was all I'd brought to his house. I looked at my simple possessions: my French press, the coffee grinder that was from my parents wedding registry. I am a minimalist, I've moved a lot. That box looked like home, and I knew I'd be okay eventually. Saying goodbye to Chloe was impossible, of course. She knew nothing of what was going on and yet she'd only know that I was gone. I left the apartment and never spoke to him again.

MY MOM WELCOMED ME INTO her house and her embrace. I was her 35-year-old baby girl, home again. As a child and teenager I'd been a total daddy's girl, but as I moved through the world on my own, and especially after my father got sick, my mom and I had become close. When I arrived at her house I saw her peer out the window as I walked up the drive—she had been waiting for me, worried. She opened the door and gave me a huge hug. I am a tall woman, much taller than my mom and yet her arms still feel like home to me. She helped me with my one bag and one box, and found a home for all my houseplants among her own.

While I was there she cooked all my favorite meals: *pasta e fagioli* and a delicious Indian curry that she'd learned to cook from her father who had been stationed in India in WWII. We'd sit around the table for an hour after dinner was over, talking and laughing and crying. My mom is in her 70s, but you'd never know it from looking at her. She's still lean and fit, a lifetime walker and hiker. We've always been physically close in appearance. Once I found a picture of myself in her house that I couldn't remember taking. When I asked her about it she told me it was actually a picture of her, taken more than 40 years ago.

When I arrived it was only a few months after the abortion, and I often wanted to discuss it with her. My mom was my first friend that I told, and those conversations helped me sort out what I was feeling and thinking as I began to approach the new landscape that lay ahead. From the beginning she had been nothing but supportive and understanding. I told her on the day of the abortion. I was in my car on my way down to the clinic, but for some reason I felt like I couldn't go through with it without her knowing. She told me she loved me and asked if there was anything she could do for me; she even offered to drive me. Her support had remained as steady ever since. Now, after the breakup, it was obvious to see that it pained her to watch me go through this, but she never got upset, no matter how hot or cold my emotions ran.

The room I stayed in was her guest room and office. I slept on a daybed—a twin—and every night when my head hit the pillow I was filled with relief. Being back in her house I slept more soundly than I had in over eight months. The room is on the small side, but beautifully outfitted in greys and blues with antique walnut furniture, and of course plants—both my mom and I have a green thumb. I felt so held by her love, and so safe in a space that felt so much like what I had grown up in.

One evening, after a particularly delicious vegetable stir fry, we sat around her small dining table, dishes waiting to be done and her two dogs snoozing in the living room while we spoke. I pushed some leftovers around my plate while my mom told me the story of one of my aunts who managed to hide an unplanned pregnancy from her entire family: my grandparents, my other aunts and uncles, and my great grandmother, who lived with them at the time. My aunt was 17 when it happened, and she didn't realize until later in her pregnancy. She was afraid to tell her parents, and with my mom away at college she felt like she had no one to turn to. I played the scenario out in my mind, unable to fathom how it was even possible to hide a pregnancy. She went into labor while my grandparents were out of town, and they got the shocking call that their daughter was having a baby. The baby was immediately given up for adoption. It was surprising for me to find out, too. It had happened decades before I was born, and by the time my mom told me I was 34. It was just one more example of a family secret kept between women, over time.

But still, the topic of pregnancy and abortion was a really uncomfortable topic for my mom to stay with. I reflected on this: my mom, who was born in the late 1940s, came of age during the Women's Liberation and Civil Rights movements. After all the gains made during that time, she had slowly seen the pendulum swing the other way to where we are now: a political climate in which abortion rights are slowly being eroded, with public sentiment on the issue in lock step. In *Choice Words*, the author Hanna Neuschwander writes about her decision to terminate a pregnancy due to the health issues of the child, and expresses her feelings about societal shame around abortion. This passage rang particularly true for me: abortion, "was the most moral decision I have ever made. Moral in the literal sense: 'concerned with the principles of right and wrong behavior and the goodness or badness of human character.' I grappled with my deepest being—my spiritual, my intellectual, my biological selves ... morality is no longer an abstract question for me. 'Right or wrong' cannot contain the scope of my moral reckoning, my moral longing. What is an acceptable level of suffering? Whose suffering matters more? Who gets to decide? No one, not even the ablest philosophers, has been able to answer these questions to our society's satisfaction. But for some reason we like to shame and vilify the very people who have grappled most viscerally with them."

My mom sat with her discomfort, for the sake of my need to process my experience. And through those conversations, I realized I didn't want to leave my abortion in the dark in my own family. If our families are a microcosm of society, then maybe we can start addressing shame at that fundamental level.

AFTER FOUR MONTHS AT MY mom's house, I was ready to move on. Both from her home, and from Arizona. In the time that the broker and I were together we had made several trips to California, and I realized that the coast was calling my name. I have always been driven to live close to nature, and the heat in Arizona largely kept me inside. I wanted to swim in the ocean, bike in the hills, and live in a smaller town once again.

While I was still learning to forgive myself for the circumstances of getting pregnant, I had a much better understanding of where the shame around it came from—that it was more from society and less from myself. The deep thinking and wrestling with my decision not only freed me up from shame, but ultimately, it reminded me of the preciousness of life. I am lucky to be here today, lucky for my health. I'm happy that in the 1980s, when I was born, my mom would have had a choice about whether or not to have me, and that I am chosen in my parent's life.

Getting out of that relationship, getting out from under the shame of my abortion made me realize how dull my life had become. I didn't want to live in shades of grey when I could be seeing everything in technicolor. I was ready to forgive myself, to love myself, and to build a life so rich and multi-faceted that every moment was worthy of being treasured.

four

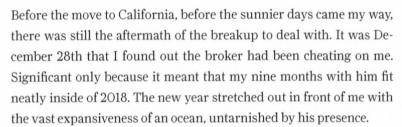

Before the move to California, before the sunnier days came my way, there was still the aftermath of the breakup to deal with. It was December 28th that I found out the broker had been cheating on me. Significant only because it meant that my nine months with him fit neatly inside of 2018. The new year stretched out in front of me with the vast expansiveness of an ocean, untarnished by his presence.

Since my early 30s I've had a habit of setting monthly intentions. I use them as a 30-day, gentle reminder to myself to bring focus to specific areas of my life. One month might be finances, and I'll read up on some corner of the investing world. Or I'll reflect on balance when I feel as though I've taken on too much between work, exercise, projects and friends. Beginning January 2019, my focus had never been so clear. I wanted to reclaim my life after finding out about the broker's infidelity and our subsequent breakup. It was the only relationship I'd had that didn't end amicably and I wanted to make sure it didn't leave a lasting dent in my psyche.

The revelation of the affair put me back on my heels again, just as I felt like I was finding my footing after the abortion. Esther Perel, in her book *State of Affairs*, explains how upon finding out about infidelity, the faithful partner suddenly realizes that they have been living in a different reality than their partner. She says, "Infidelity is a direct attack on one of our most important psychic structures: our memory of the past ... If we can't look back with any certainty and we can't know what will happen tomorrow, where does that leave us?" And in my case, realizing that my intuition had been right made it all the more frustrating. Perel, again: "Sometimes the corrosive torment of doubting a partner's fidelity is made worse by the cruel practice of gaslighting," Perel continues, "... now she feels doubly betrayed. He made her doubt not just him, but her own sanity." These words spoke my truth. I was trying to suss out fact from fiction in my past, and to remember there was nothing for me to be ashamed of. At the same time, I was struggling not to be mad at myself for working so hard to trust someone who was not worthy of my trust and confidence.

I spoke to my life coach Laila the morning after I walked out of his house for good. I called her from my mom's blue and grey guest bedroom, sitting on the neatly made bed. The sound of my mom's wind chimes drifted in through the window, and I looked up to see green palo verde trees stirred by a gentle breeze. My new normal had not yet sunk in—the situation felt surreal, like I was an outsider, looking in. Laila wanted me to focus on what she called Radical Self-Care, meaning this week I could give myself whatever I felt I needed, whenever I needed it. At the time of our conversation, I didn't see how indulging myself with massages and takeout was entirely necessary, nor did I see how such "frivolous" things could be self-care. Typically, I think of self-care as pertaining to the realm of sleep, nutrition, mindfulness, and exercise. But as reality set in and I began to feel the full range of emotions that came with a breakup—sadness, anger, elation—I realized she had tossed me a life ring as I began to drift in a sea of feelings.

As the ups and downs set in, mere fundamentals of self-care felt woefully inadequate. I learned that love isn't something that can be turned off like a light switch, even in the case of infidelity. Despite his flaws, I had loved him. He challenged me intellectually, took the time to get to know my friends and family, and included me in his social circle as well. We talked about the future, and that feeling of building something together had felt binding. I found myself at once in love

with him, hating him, and even *missing him*. All the while I was re-
pulsed by the thought of him with other women. I wanted to disinfect
my body, swish my mouth with bleach— anything to get that crawling
feeling off my skin. In the end, I had to learn to live with all of it. The
love, the hate, the disgust. It came in waves—good memories swallowed up by a moment of rage, a yearning to call him pushed away
by the memory of the texts I found in his phone. The extra self-care
indulgences wouldn't be necessary forever, but they partially filled a
hole where our relationship had been and let me know my love for
myself was enough.

I spent hours on end reading in the bathtub, re-upping the hot
water as it turned tepid. I finished several books in there, candles lit
and the bathroom fan on. The white noise and the stories allowed me
to escape my own reality, giving my body and mind a break from the
emotional push and pull between elation and grief. I listened to music
on repeat: Beethoven's symphonies seemed to understand my sadness, the *Frozen* soundtrack brought me empowerment, Jason DeRu-
lo and Adele captured the essence of infidelity. I splurged on several
massages in one month and saw my acupuncturist, who had been
through so much with me at this point. I ate an entire chocolate bar
as a part of my dinner one night. Simple or extravagant, I gave myself
whatever my body or my psyche wanted.

I discovered that, rather than feeling gluttonous or guilty, these
simple acts created pockets of tenderness toward myself. In those
spaces I found I could imagine a future so much brighter than the
life I had been living. I would journal about the home I dreamed of
making for myself and I could feel the idea beginning to take root in
my being. I could envision simple things: a window with a view of
trees outside, an oriental rug on a hardwood floor, a pastel sunrise, my
boyfriend's board shorts in our closet. I put sounds and smells to my
dreams to make them come to life: the sound of a fountain outside my
window, coffee with that same boyfriend in the morning, the smell of

puppy feet from the dog sleeping on my side of the bed.

This dream of a happy future slowly crowded out the intrusive thoughts I still suffered from. Those thoughts would still creep up on me out of the blue: *he cheated on me*, and always, *I had an abortion*. My heart rate would spike and adrenaline would leave my skin tingling, like I'd been splashed with too-hot water. They popped in when I was hiking my favorite trail, miles from another soul, or in a dusty used bookstore. I'd find myself emptied, wondering: how I could justify feeling hopeful about my future when my "freedom" had come at so great a cost? As I began to heal, I came to realize that the only justification for the price of the abortion was to live a life of value to myself. Beginning to build on that dream I had written about, slowly, slowly crowded out any remnants of my old relationship.

AROUND THE TIME OF MY birthday—t-minus one month to VC (victory over cheating) day, and five months before I made the move to California—I was planning a solo trip to New Zealand to meet some old friends. At the time, the vacation had a *get me the hell out of here!* feel to it. The trip was going to be three weeks—two on the South Island, and one on the North Island. I'd use up all of my vacation time at work and even go into the red a bit, but I had a reputation as a dependable employee and they greenlit the extra days off without question.

I was still with the broker when I booked my ticket. Although I desperately wanted to break up with him, I was still in the place where I didn't know how to walk away and didn't think I had the strength to stay away if I did. All signs still pointed to us staying together—we were making Thanksgiving and Christmas plans, and the broker wanted to buy some furniture together. That said, I secretly hoped that I'd be single by the time I went on the trip in February. Despite my desire to leave, a deeply rooted habit of being a nice girlfriend meant I spent hours at work with a browser window open as I considered buying a ticket for him to come with me. In a small act of good girl rebellion, I never booked the ticket; I was going solo.

My unlikely hopes (but wildest dreams) came true. Come February I was single (though not yet resettled in California) and pleased as punch to be so. Counting the days until my flight, I knew my intention for the coming month. I wanted to have *fun*. Moving on from recovery mode and into this happier space felt like real progress.

My first stop was a couple of weeks on the South Island, meeting up with a friend of 12 years and her boyfriend for some backpacking and packrafting adventures. My trip began in Christchurch where I took a bus to a local Kathmandu outdoors store (similar to REI here in the States) where I needed to pick up one or two forgotten items, and where Ella and Steve would come to pick me up in their car. On the bus ride, I looked around: New Zealand could not have been further from Arizona. The city was green, and still recovering from the earthquake back in 2011. Shipping containers had been turned into stores or restaurants after buildings had come down. Colorful murals covered their corrugated walls.

Ella and her boyfriend picked me up in their small van, and I dozed as we left town and climbed up and up a windy mountain road to Arthur's Pass National Park. We camped there for the night so that we could make our way to the west coast in the morning. I woke up to a chill mist and low clouds. Wandering out of my tent I marveled at our modern world: one day I was in the dry, harsh Sonoran desert with a wide open sky, the next I was in the Southern Hemisphere, heading to a tropical forest.

During our first few days together, Ella and I didn't really talk about my relationship, though she knew I'd left the broker. Then we left for a girls-only overnight backpacking trip. As Steve drove off down a dusty road leaving us at the trailhead, I knew we'd finally have a chance to discuss what really happened. We had a several mile hike out to a small one-room cabin maintained by New Zealand's Department of Conservation, geared specifically to backpackers. We started off hiking on a hilly farmstead and then tramped over a forested ridge before getting a break. It was sunny and humid and there wasn't much talking happening those first hours. Finally, as we descended into a forested valley, Ella asked to hear the story.

As I pondered where to begin I looked around; the hillsides were so green they practically glowed, full of exotic plants and ferns, populated by colorful birds. The air was thick with humidity, and the birds loud— it was a truly wild place. This trip was not just a break from the desert, but it was also giving me a break from what had become the anxious narrative of my life. It was too soon to tell her everything, and I was too raw. I knew my friend would be supportive, but I also knew I would struggle to take in her thoughts or opinions about the situation with a level head, however well-intentioned her reaction may have been.

By this point we had reached a riverbed studded with Volkswagen-sized white boulders. The teal green water slipped between the rocks and was crystal clear and freezing cold. I told her what I could bear, but I didn't mention the abortion. I cited general differences in life goals as our problem, and blamed his limited emotional intelligence from keeping us moving forward. She sensed my hesitation and let the subject drop. We made it to the hut, using a rope bridge to cross a wide flat river that was the last obstacle before reaching our home for the night. As Ella prepared her dinner, I stretched out on a top bunk looking out the window. The sun had set and the skies were shades of perfect purples and blues. I lay there journaling, wondering when I'd be ready to tell her. Not tonight, not this trip. There was a certain relief in giving myself permission to take a break from the whole thing.

I have since had the conversation with Ella. About nine months after my New Zealand trip we met up in Utah for some mountain biking. She and Steve were digital nomads, spending summers in the US traveling the West Coast and traveling to New Zealand for northern hemisphere winters. I told her both about the cheating and about the abortion, and she was blindsided. The look on her face was almost comical and her head rocked back as though she had been physically hit by my statement. *You? But you're so careful, so on top of everything!* I was nervous telling her and ploughed on with the details. After it was all out she asked how I was doing—how I was *really* doing.

I told her how hard it had been to tell people the truth. I explained that I couldn't tell her in New Zealand because I still felt so exposed, and I needed a break from my feelings while I figured out what the whole thing meant to me. She was understanding, and expressed her relief—she had felt the tension between us during our trip and had worried it was somehow her doing. I told her I was grateful for our friendship and how she had helped me during that time, even if she didn't know she was doing it. Trying to make meaning of a situation like this—one that has caused so much inner conflict—takes time and space and self-compassion. Our time adventuring in the Kiwi bush helped remind me that there was so much more to my life than *that*. Not having to be a *woman who had an abortion* for those couple of weeks, being reminded of a different version of myself, helped me integrate those two pieces. I am my nature-loving, laughing self, and I am a person who at some point found her way out of a sticky situation.

DURING THAT TRIP TO NEW Zealand, I also had the opportunity to catch up with another longtime friend. Catherine and I hadn't seen each other for close to seven years. The last time we had hung out was when we were both still living in Colorado, and she was about to return to New Zealand, where she was originally from. From my vantage point back then, she was living a fulfilling life. She was about a year out of her divorce and was living in a sunny apartment with her black and white border collie, Dusty. She was running a lot and her work as a massage therapist was keeping her busy. She had seemed so settled for so long that I was a little surprised to learn that she would be leaving the States.

One day during my visit, we were taking a trip north to an inlet on the coast with calm enough water for paddling and diverse bird and sea life. On the drive she told me that there was more to the end of her time in Colorado than met the eye. It turns out that after her divorce she had fallen into a relationship with a locally famous mountaineer. He was handsome, successful and had long been unattached, given his packed travel schedule. It had been a fairy tale romance, but it was short and ended in heartbreak for her when he wanted to return to his single life of travel and ice climbing. She was on her own Ferris wheel of life, from down to up and back again. After that relationship she felt adrift and confused about who she was and what to do with this new self of hers. It felt so much like my own story.

Day after day in New Zealand I witnessed Catherine happy and whole again: living in the embrace of her parents and siblings, mountain biking, paddling and running every day, and in love again with someone new. It was life affirming to me. I could feel myself opening up, my posture straightening, chest and face pointing upward like a flower opening to the sun. One afternoon on her patio, we chatted long after we finished eating a late lunch. Her Chihuahua Rufus (Dusty stayed behind on the move from the US) was sitting on her lap and we both had our feet up in chairs. Though it was midday, the trees provided shade from the sun and we happily lingered outside. We were talking more about her journey to where she was today, and it helped me remember that I too had been through adversity before. I recalled one hard year in my late 20s, in which my dad received his diagnosis, I left a five-year relationship, and my dog passed away. Back then I never could have imagined that someday I would feel as strong and content as I felt sitting on Catherine's patio. I had gotten out of my relationship and was building the life I wanted, if slowly. I realized I hadn't come this far, only to come this far.

Dr. Tomaino, the neuropsychologist who wrote *Awakening the Brain*, says that when she works with patients, "If I can grasp their desire and make my vision real to them with the certainty of what I have seen, I become the bridge to where they want to go." I felt like Catherine was doing just that for me. Being in sunny, green New Zealand, knowing what she had been through and seeing with my own eyes what a happy place she wound up in, was the medicine I needed most. Catherine became my bridge by modeling the type of life I wanted for myself.

Our week together cemented my desire to make some changes when I got home. One day we paddled up a tributary on the eastern coast, where we saw hundreds of stingrays within reach under our boards. They were several feet across and flew under the water, so many of them at once that they were nearly indistinguishable from one another. Another day we went mountain biking on the western coast—in the span of one morning it was sunny and hot and then drizzly and cool. We rode up and down forested hills, and later along cliffs overlooking the ocean. We ate at a hip vegan restaurant with a cliff side view and flowers topping our salads. I met her brothers and parents, saw how she'd transformed her job, and found out for myself just how cool her new boyfriend was. Her return to herself moved something within me. I was still living in Arizona at the time, and she was the first person I told that I wanted to move to California, a card I'd held close to my chest so far. It seemed so audacious that I was afraid to broadcast it; I didn't want to face embarrassment if I failed. When she dropped me off at the airport she promised to visit me in my new home.

My flight home from Auckland was 12 sleepless hours long. The cabin was cold and dark for the majority of the flight and I was in a middle seat, covered in blankets. The man in the seat next to me chewed his nails incessantly as the plane veered north and south, higher and lower in altitude, avoiding storms over an ocean as restless as my soul. I knew I wanted to take the leap and leave Arizona but the idea of actually doing it terrified me. Between the nervous energy from my seat mate, the turbulence, and my own anxiety at the thought of returning to my old life in Arizona, there was a choke hold on my neck and a vice grip on my heart. After what seemed like a lifetime, the plane began to descend into the LA basin. The sunlight played on the white-capped waves of the Pacific, and once the wheels touched down my anxiety seemed to evaporate.

Like the ground beneath me, my resolve to make whatever changes necessary to live the life I wanted solidified. I rushed off the plane in the newly remodeled international terminal at LAX. The high ceilings and full-length windows of the building were a welcome relief after the dark confines of the cabin. The terminal was nearly empty, and I knew I had a long walk to my next gate, but I had something to do first. I found the nearest bench and sat down to use the airport WiFi. I emailed my life coach: I was moving to California. I knew the kind of town I was looking for: somewhere close to nature, with a strong sense of community and a decent job scene. It was still early in the year, and 2019 was looking up.

AND SO IT WAS, ONE sunny day, that I drove from Arizona to California in a clunky U-Haul box truck. I rolled into my new town with Kygo pumping out from the stereo, palm trees and taco shops lining the streets. Arriving in this new place felt like coming home, as though I had been on this path for so long, but hadn't been able to see it yet. It was my own *renaissance*, a rebirth, a chance to see the world through new eyes. I was on my way.

I spent my first two months in California subletting the top-level room and loft of a three-bedroom house about a 20-minute walk from downtown. I was sharing the home with two inspiring young women—a journalist and a scientist both researching climate change—one an avid paddler racing with a local outrigger canoeing team, the other a talented painter. The man whose room I was staying in was a software developer, away for a few months in Argentina. For the first time in what felt like forever, my life felt uncomplicated and safe. My window was open, and a Pacific breeze blew across my bare arms. My view was of a green hillside, dotted with houses, purple mountains farther in the distance. I was bowled over with a sense of relief, my life unfolding on what felt like its right trajectory again at last.

But old habits (and thought patterns) die hard, and one morning as I was puttering around my temporary new home, I found myself wondering once again *how I could be so stupid as to get pregnant*, when my brother called. Despite having made friends with my new roommates, I still spent a fair amount of time solo on the weekends. I usually managed to avoid spending that time ruminating, but that day his call was a pleasant interruption.

My brother is a Jesuit, which means he is a member of the Society of Jesus—a Catholic religious community best known for their involvement in education. Pope Francis is a Jesuit. My brother is like Pope Francis, if Francis were 37, mustachioed and often found eating gelato in downtown Los Angeles. For the past two years his ministry had seen him doing regular projects that took his full attention and kept him from calling with any regularity. On the day of our call, he was acting as a hospital chaplain in South Central LA. Other projects he'd been involved with included building housing in a remote town in Alaska, and taking part in a month-long silent retreat. I could hear the smile on his face as he greeted me, and it was like an instant over-the-air hug.

My brother is 18 months older than I am. We moved frequently when we were growing up and we were often each other's only friends. As we got older, he made high school bearable for me since I was shy to the point of awkwardness. As I fumbled my way through college, he always supported and accepted me exactly where I was. We joke about sibling ESP all the time, but it's true; he understands me in a way that no one else does. As we talked, I sat in a sunny spot on my couch mindlessly tugging on a thread that had come undone from my jean shorts.

I explained to him how hard it was for me to be around people, particularly new people, that I hadn't really opened up to yet here in

California. They saw me the same as everyone does, warm and compassionate. *But if they knew about the abortion, they might not want to be friends with me!* I told him. I could picture myself as Wylie Coyote in the cartoon, my new friends acting like Roadrunner—legs spinning like a pinwheel before leaving me coughing in the dust.

My brother counseled me to open my mind, and, as impossible as it seemed, set aside any stories I had on repeat in my head: like me being unlovable. The sound of his voice was calming to me, with the measured cadence learned from more than a decade as a college professor. He told me I had two options: *continue to beat myself up and believe my thoughts, or choose a more constructive path.* Maybe I could see this as an opportunity to help other women who were going through a shitty hard time. Maybe I could imagine it was the push I'd needed to change my life for the better (as I'd already started to do). Ground I'd gone over with my life coach, but for some reason, coming from him, I understood it in a different way. Not only could I look at my life in a different way, but I could also live it in a different way. My life was a choose-your-own-adventure novel; I could decide if I wanted to grow from this experience or stay stalled in a world of self-inflicted suffering.

All the great spiritual teachers believe this. Pain is inevitable; suffering is optional. There will be hardship and loss in our lives, but it is how we respond to it that determines how long and to what depth we have negative feelings. On the one hand we can act on our emotions by getting angry, raging, sobbing; on the other we can ignore and repress everything we feel, turning to some kind of escape mechanism. As long as we cling to the negative narratives we write in our head, we will continue to agonize over the event by lashing out or repressing. The third option is to sit with the feeling, let it pass. To look at the event in a clear-headed state and pick your story, rather than allowing a story to pick you. I had an abortion, yes. It surely caused physical pain, grief, and it forced a change in my life and the life of those around me. However, deciding that I was unlovable because of this was my own choice. In repeating this narrative, I had been wiring my brain to believe it, to choose suffering when I didn't have to.

I understood his reasoning and agreed with it. But I felt like it completely ignored the existential question around abortion: did I take a life? It had taken me months to ask these questions of myself. I asked him point blank what he thought. *Did I take a life? Did I stop a soul from coming into existence? What does that make me?* I wasn't afraid to ask him, nor was I afraid of his answer. He has always been loving-ly, completely honest with me. He told me he didn't have a direct an-swer—that he didn't feel these questions even had answers, and may-be were the wrong questions to begin with. Instead, he offered this: *We are wretches, but beloved wretches. We are sinners, but beloved sinners.* I could spend my life trying to answer these questions, or I could get on with it and I could take this as an opportunity to shape the decisions I make in the future. It reminded me of something I read by Gloria Stei-nem; the doctor who performed her abortion made her promise, "that you will do what you want with your life." My brother was giving me the same sage advice.

Something clicked into place: it would be a waste of my life, *and* it would dishonor that child-that-never-was, for me to stay trapped in a negative story of my own making. My only course of action going forward was to make every second count. To be of service to others where and when I could, which started with helping myself.

We riffed on this theme for another ten minutes, but then our con-versation shifted. I stood up and walked around the room, getting life back into my legs. He made a joke that I was getting old and we both got a good chuckle out of it. The atmosphere shifted and the mood was lighter. We made plans to see each other soon and discussed where we wanted to meet for Christmas. Talked about how we could help our mom care for our ailing dad more easily. Am I a woman who had an abortion? Yes. A monster? Maybe. But a sister, and a daughter, and beloved.

five

~

There is another element to this story, one that adds a layer of complexity that I found myself grappling with after the broker and I split up. The broker was a foreign national, born on an island in the Caribbean. Dating him was the first time I had been in a relationship with someone outside of my own race. It was also the beginning of a journey of learning and unlearning, and an opportunity to find out more about another culture and another side of my own country. It has been (and continues to be) a humbling experience, with lots of missteps, but ultimately it is a journey I'm grateful to take part in.

One evening early in our relationship, I was sitting on the couch in his apartment while we were chatting after dinner—Chloe resting her head on my knee, hoping for some attention. He was doing the dishes in his usual methodical manner—soap, stack, rinse—while he told me a story. During his undergraduate years here in the States, a young woman wanted to interview him about his experience as an African American man at college. He recounted to me his efforts to explain to her that because he was not American, he could not be African American, and did not identify as such. No matter how he explained his identity to her—that he identified as a Black man—she just couldn't, or wouldn't, wrap her head around it. How could this person decide for him how he wanted to be identified? What did she know about his journey to get here? I could see how strong this memory was with him, almost like he was back there with her, trying in vain to explain himself all over again. He turned his focus back to me and asked if I understood what he meant.

This was typical of how the broker handled conversations like these: using a story to gently explain to me "please do this, and don't do that." He was kind to me when I made missteps. This was my first foray into facing and understanding the concept of race as it pertains to privilege, and he treated me in a way that was consistent with how he chose to view everyone when it came to race: that on the whole, people were not trying to be malicious when they acted or spoke from a place of unconscious racial bias, they were simply ignorant of the correct way to behave, and often too afraid to ask.

I wanted to make my relationship work, and knew navigating this would be fundamental to us. Early in our relationship, the broker explained to me that I exhibited "colorblindness"—a term I hadn't heard up until that point in my life. In her book *Me and White Supremacy*, author and teacher Layla Saad clearly spells out why colorblindness can be attractive for those of us unsure about how to navigate race, and why it is so damaging. "The promise of the Church of Color Blindness is that if we stop seeing race, then racism goes away." Of course, "the problem does not go away because you refuse to see it. And this kind of thinking is naive at best and dangerous at worst." This was eye-opening to me, both with regard to my relationship, and the world at large. Because I was unsure about how to talk about race with the broker, I did what I thought was best and treated him the same way I'd treat anyone else. Which was to say, without drawing attention to the difference in the color of our skin. I abided by his request to describe him as being "Black," though the occasion never arose for me to use the term in public. When the topic did come up between the two of us, the word stuck in my throat, like I was being forced to be edgy or worldly in a way that I just wasn't. But I didn't want to be like the woman interviewing him that time, and had to learn to sit with my discomfort. The education that he was giving me made me realize it was high time more of us (us being white people) learned to be uncomfortable for the sake of dismantling the white supremacy that has such deep and insidious roots in our country.

My relationship with a man of color—being emotionally and physically intimate with him, navigating the world outside with him—revealed to me many of my blind spots, and made me realize that there were undoubtedly many more lurking, waiting to be uncovered. It made me see white privilege in a broader, systemic way, and opened my eyes to a million daily injustices faced by people in this country. I felt humbled and naive.

It was around two months into our relationship (still three months away from when I became pregnant) that I began to consider that any child we had together would be mixed race. This brought up a question for me: how would I have a conversation with my child about something I had never experienced? I remember being young myself, and being angry when my parents just didn't understand. I could imagine a child of mine being frustrated when I tried to work through issues surrounding race with them. I had never been judged or discriminated against for the color of my skin. I did a lot of internet research about this and the internet was not nearly as kind with me as the broker had been.

In an odd twist of fate, this question worried me right up until I became pregnant. Once confronted with the reality of becoming co-parents, our relationship took a turn towards a town called Nowhere Good and the topic of race seemed secondary—we needed to know if we'd even continue the pregnancy, if we'd stay together, where we'd live ... the list felt endless. I wanted to be a mother so badly. And though I was unsure if the broker would be good father material, I had faith he would be able to help with these tough conversations should the situation arise.

Our relationship is long in the past now, but the journey I began back then to understand my own relationship with race, and how racial bias breeds systemic injustice, is just beginning. It has taught me to question why I hold some of the stereotypes I do (inside and outside of race, even), and has forced me to face hard truths about myself. I make mistakes, I try to correct myself gently, as he did, and I keep going.

ABOUT A MONTH AFTER BREAKING up with the broker, my friend at the office—the one who counseled me when I found the broker's cheerleader avatar—outlined all the reasons my breakup was for the best. She believed that "once a cheater always a cheater," and also pointed out I wouldn't have the worry and judgment that came with raising mixed-race children. Her statement gave me pause. Racism is not a thing of the past, but I felt like in my friend group a mixed-race child would be accepted without judgment or question. I challenged her on this, and she expounded that although our friend group would have supported me, unconscious racial bias in the world at large would have put my child at a serious disadvantage. Touché. Being the ultimate devil's advocate, she couldn't help but bring up one last question: was I certain this bias hadn't played into my decision to terminate the pregnancy? Her perfectly shaped right eyebrow raised itself into a question mark.

Wait, what? I brought this question with me to my therapist the next time I saw him. Noah repeated my own question back to me to gauge my reaction to my own words: did I think race played a part in my decision? I sat on his faded brown couch, eyes closed, fingers tracing the piping on the edge of the cushion, my mind chasing the thoughts as they swirled through my head—curling and twisting like cream just added to hot coffee. Well? I didn't think so. It had never occurred to me before. Having a mixed-race child would have been challenging in some ways certainly, but the race of the child was never part of the equation during my wrangling with the decision to terminate the pregnancy. It was always about the broker's ability to be a good partner and father, and my judgment of right and wrong, moral and amoral.

I'd been seeing Noah for several months by this point. He had been recommended to me by a friend, and I didn't expect anything outside of normal talk therapy when I went in to see him. I was surprised to find out how many other modalities he had incorporated into his practice, including the dream work we had done previously, somatic psychology and energy work. Not something I expected to find in the office of a male, white-haired, Christian practitioner.

Both somatic psychology and energy work focus on the physical body. Using our own flesh and energetic systems, we can uncover previously inaccessible information about our pasts, and the truths living in our subconscious. Once we can access what's there, we can use our own body or energy to release old hurts and unhealthy habits or patterns, and heal. On my first session with Noah he had me hold out my dominant arm, level with the floor. He asked me my name while pushing down on my arm. It barely budged. He asked me to say a fictitious name while doing the same thing. My arm bottomed out. When standing in my truth, my body was strong. When thinking a non-truth, my body would weaken.

Noah had used this technique consistently in our sessions, though I didn't always want to hear the messages coming from my body. Like when he uncovered some lack of self-worth in a hidden corner of my soul. In his office I discovered my fears about being 35 and single, and how this might lead me to be alone forever. I realized that if I really believed in my value and capability, I'd have been ready to leave the broker, knowing there was someone out there who would be worthy of my love. Noah's BS meter was flawless.

The day I arrived in his office with my question about race, I was curious (and maybe a little worried) about what I might find out. I know we all are infected with unconscious racial bias, but could any societal conditioning have become so deeply ingrained in me to have impacted my relationship with my own unborn child? As I knew he would, Noah eventually asked me to put out my arm. Did the broker's race have anything to do with my decision to terminate the pregnancy? He pushed down and my arm held firm. The answer: my decision to terminate the pregnancy was not due to race. Our session continued, and we talked about it some more.

I wanted to believe my body, but I went home feeling like I had only half an answer. I knew on a conscious level that race had not come up in the calculus I used to decide to have an abortion. But what if it had come up unconsciously? I knew I would not be satisfied until I could unpack the issue in a more logical way. My question nagged at me in quiet moments until one day I was lying on my stomach journaling (as one does), taking up every corner of my mom's single guest bed. I found myself wishing that I'd become pregnant by a different ex. Any other ex. With them, I wouldn't have had an abortion and wouldn't be here wondering about my morals, I reasoned. Well, any ex except one of them, I thought, I'd never in a million years have had a kid with *him* either. A lightbulb turned on.

I sat up, realizing my mind had presented me with another way to tackle the issue about race. I quickly ran through the list of past boyfriends and asked myself what would have happened with any of them, had I become pregnant while we were together. I was able to rattle off the list in seconds: my first boyfriend, I'd have kept a child with him for sure; the cyclist, same; the soccer player ... Yikes. There it was. In a half a heartbeat I knew that had we become pregnant together, I would have terminated that pregnancy as well. He was nice, handsome, funny, but a complete train wreck in terms of finances and the most insecure person I'd dated. He was also white.

Just months before this exercise, uncovering that I was indeed open to having an abortion would have horrified me. Today, it was able to bring me peace of mind about my decision. It didn't ease the general onslaught of emotions that I still felt on a daily basis: grief, guilt, and regret tugged me this way and that, often making it hard to complete tasks in my day-to-day life without a break to go cry or yell my rage into a pillow. But this simple thought exercise confirmed that my decision came from a desire for a better life for myself, and to protect my child from the traumas of growing up in a shattered home, with parents who lived by completely different value systems. It brought me peace to know that the broker being Black had nothing to do with my decision to terminate the pregnancy.

THAT QUESTION HAS LONG BEEN set aside for me, as have many of the other things that made me feel guilty about my decision. But guilt is such a complex emotion. It's like a brilliant cut diamond with its many facets: some small and some large, flat and white in this light, a rainbow of color when twisted the other way, all waiting to reflect your soul back at you at every turn.

I caught another glimpse of myself—the version who thought she should be wracked with guilt for what she did—while reading Elie Wiesel's *Night*. The book is a Holocaust memoir, and in it Elie recounts the story of his dad calling out to him while he was dying. Elie didn't leave his bunk and wished his father would be quiet because his calls would only bring around the SS guards. He says that he will never forgive himself for not going to his father; and worse, that his thoughts were of self-preservation in that pivotal moment. He felt like when the time came, he didn't pass "the test"—he put his own safety ahead of the needs of his dying father. His story gave me the sense that he thought this made him the worst person in the world. When I read that passage, it jumped out at me and I sat up straight. My fingers retraced the text. I've got you beat, I thought. I also didn't pass the test.

Even if we don't face a traumatic life event, like the death of our father in a concentration camp or the weight of a child lost to abortion, we all carry guilt from our imperfectly lived lives. I am responsible for the inadvertent death of a hamster when I was around six years old. My mom accidentally slammed my brother's head in a car door on a sunny afternoon when he was about the same age. The episode left her so shaken she still can't talk about it. Parents miss softball games and swim practices, people hide behind little white lies, spouses cheat after too many glasses of wine at a sales conference. As humans, we make mistakes, often at the same exact time we're trying our best, and we all feel guilt for the pain and anguish those mistakes cause.

Intentional or unintentional, these are the things we carry, and they will eat away at us unless we find a way to face them, forgive ourselves, and set them aside. People turn to addictions—destructive or more benign—to repress the more painful memories. Others will be less impacted, but won't live the fullest extent of their lives with this weight hanging over them. Thich Nhat Hanh argues that guilt can help us recognize the bad things we have done, but that it isn't good to be locked in guilt, saying, "You can do something to neutralize the wrong deed in the past ... and after you have made that vow within your heart, the transformation and healing begins to take place." The deeds are not to be forgotten but placed safely out of the way of our future, so our journey forward is not impeded, and instead elevated and directed by the lessons we've learned.

Guilt is also very individual because it is dependent on each of our own unique moral codes. What we feel guilty for can be strongly influenced by our society, religions, and family. What in one culture is taboo may be normal in another. If someone in our family was affected by an event, it may be something that is high on our radar to avoid, whereas someone less close to the issue would pay it less mind.

My sense of guilt is certainly tied up in all of those factors. American views on abortion run the gamut, but there is a segment of society that considers abortion murder. In *Without Apology*, Jenny Brown explains how these views infiltrate our society: "Those who feel bad, sad, guilty, regretful or grief stricken about their abortions are given plenty of encouragement for these feelings. In fact, anti-abortion forces try to make every woman feel so guilty, sinful, selfish and ashamed that she won't have an abortion in the first place." Reading this made me realize that my emotional reaction to my abortion could be in part due to unconscious anti-abortion bias. It was eye-opening to me.

Beyond American society, I looked at my family and personal background with abortion. I come from a largely religious family, though not strict in any real sense. Throughout my pregnancy my mother and brother (both Catholic) never questioned me or my choices; they held me and loved me unconditionally. That said, I have attended masses in which priests have said prayers for the souls of aborted children. And in one startling incident, I attended a mass in which the parish priest lauded the fact that he and some supporters were able to shut down an abortion clinic via protesting. That was the last time I visited that particular church.

The bottom line is that our guilt largely depends on the lens through which we see the world. When I ask myself Elie's question today—"did I pass the test?"— I now have the ability to observe which lens I am choosing when I answer. If I choose to believe that I stopped a life in its tracks, and leave out the context, then yes, of course I feel guilty. If I choose to believe that I spared a child, and myself, lives of difficulty and unhappiness, then I can ask myself the question and answer with certainty: yes, I passed the test.

BEING ABLE TO FORM DIFFERENT lenses through which I saw my guilt began with me getting clear on what I was responsible for, and, equally, what I was not responsible for. Yes, I got pregnant unintentionally, but I was hardly alone when it happened. Jenny Brown addresses this very issue in Without Apology: "Behind every abortion is a man who didn't wear a condom ... When abortion is discussed, he fades out of the picture, while her sexual activities and her 'failure to take precautions' are picked over in detail. His sexual activities or failure to use birth control are rarely considered." If the broker had been more open to condoms, or had followed through on our agreement to use the withdrawal method, maybe I wouldn't have to ask this question of myself at all. Yes, I was responsible; no, the responsibility was not all mine.

It took me a long time to form these thoughts. For the first year after the abortion I considered it entirely my fault. I thought I was solely to blame. I took myself to the clinic, I asked for the pills, I swallowed them. Of my own volition. I am the person who had unprotected sex, I chose to stay in the bad relationship that led me there, and I am the one who chose to ignore my intuition and date an openly misogynistic man in the first place.

These faults—my weakness, my stupidity, my irresponsibility— they tormented me. I was on the phone with Laila one day, chasing blame and shame along a well-worn path in my mind when I paused mid-tirade. I was halfway through a thought when the furies in my head silenced all at once. In the space that followed, I tipped my head to the side as a new idea began to form. I was not the only player in this drama. It was as though the current I had been floating down was shrouded in fog and suddenly the sky cleared, illuminating a dynamic river of differing widths and breadths, rapids and flat water. There was more to this story that, in my grief, I hadn't been able to see.

For example, zooming out beyond just my or the broker's role in this, who is to blame for the fact that we don't have better male birth control options? We've been controlling the female reproductive system for centuries. We have cures for some forms of cancer. We have HIV meds so potent that they can make a person appear negative on a test for a disease that, only three decades ago, carried a death sentence. Humans landed on the moon in 1969, and you're telling me that we haven't come up with a better form of male birth control than ... condoms? The American Medical Association *Journal of Ethics* says:

"On the whole, female methods tend to be more expensive than male methods ... In addition to being more expensive, female methods have more serious side effects than male methods, in part because various contraceptive methods for women involve hormones, while no methods for men do. The most common reason women discontinue contraceptive use is unwanted side effects, and most forms of contraception have discontinuation rates approaching 50 percent after one year of use. Finally, the two available male forms of contraception, condoms and vasectomy, also carry fewer health risks than their corresponding female methods, female barrier contraceptives and tubal ligation."

Maybe if male birth control had been available to us, or had even been available in a past relationship, giving me a break from two decades of a medication half of women don't make it more than one year on, then I would not have found myself the villain of this story. Was the patriarchy to blame?

And what about the broker's own addictions, and his deeply rooted sexist beliefs? Were these things "his fault," or were they the result of a traumatic childhood? His father had an extramarital affair, resulting in a child outside his marriage and established family. The broker himself had wished for years that his mother would leave his father. Though his father softened as he aged, the broker told me that emotional abuse and neglect were a part of daily life growing up. Is it any wonder that he had committed some of the same mistakes he had seen on repeat during his childhood? Like a record player skipping endlessly, unable to move forward in the song. I wanted that baby. Had he not had so many underlying issues of his own around fatherhood, perhaps he would have wanted it too. Was his broken home to blame?

And what about my own family? I was raised in a household in which my mother's voice and opinion was only of value when it mirrored that of my father's. Like so many women of her generation, her role was mainly to keep him happy and the household on an even keel. In my own relationship, I prioritized the broker's sexual desires above my own common sense. I trusted his stories over my intuition when I suspected him of cheating. I wish that gender equality had been better modeled for me at home. If anything, the abortion taught me that my needs and wants are of equal importance to any man's.

Was gender inequality to blame?

Reviewing all the players in this story, today I have a much clearer picture of what led to my decision. Maybe it was everybody's fault, and no one person was to blame.

IN THIS POLITICALLY-VOLATILE, EVER-CHANGING, reactive, religious, and emotionally stunted world of ours, a lot of people still seem to think the "answer" to abortion is to control women's bodies. And as much as a world without abortion would be ideal, it is doubtful that the need for this procedure will ever go away—and certainly not because of a bunch of laws made by privileged, white men.

Though often painted as an issue of religion and morality, there are also those who argue that these laws in fact stem from the need of an ever-growing economy, and thus the need for an ever-growing workforce to bolster that economy. Further, Katha Pollitt, in *Reclaiming Abortion Rights*, explains that reproductive rights "are not a distraction from the important, economic issues. They are an economic issue: without the ability to limit and time their pregnancies, women will always be disadvantaged at work and subordinate to men." Simply put, abortion allows women "to only have children they want and can raise well."

For women to truly achieve economic equality, both men and women need to have equal stakes in child raising. Ideally, this would mean equal, paid, parental leave from work, as in Sweden, where parents are given a total of 480 days to split between them, of which 90 each go to the man or woman exclusively and cannot be transferred to the other partner. As long as women are unable to plan their pregnancies, and men are not given more time off to care for children, women will fall behind at work and remain disadvantaged in the workplace. The secondary effect of this is that ultimately women will remain economically behind, which means we will continue to depend on men to some degree.

As long as there are unwanted pregnancies (remember, that's 50 percent of all pregnancies in the US), women should have the right to do as they need—for their futures, for their bodies, and for their own security. How can it be right that this decision is forced on us by lawmakers and politicians, who know and care nothing for the individual circumstances of the human lives at stake?

The unborn children of abortion—the lives that are at the real heart of this issue—must also be counted in this equation. How many unplanned for children are born into lives of seemingly intractable inequality? When the Alabama Human Life Protection Act was signed in 2019, Governor Kay Ivy ended her statement on the draconian law (which aims for a near wholesale ban on abortion): "We must give every person the best chance for a quality life and a promising future." No matter that Alabama is the sixth poorest state in the US, with 17.2% of Alabamians living below the poverty line (the national average is 14%). Given that the people most likely to be affected by this law are also the poorest—those who lack widespread access to healthcare and birth control, leading them to abortion in the first place—many souls entering the world as a result of this bill will be pre-destined for a life of poverty-induced suffering.

And then there is the complicated, often contradictory debate about the role of race in abortion. In a *New York Times* article from 2019, John Eligon says, "Those seeking to outlaw abortion lament what they see as an undoing of the fabric of Black families. They liken the high abortion rates among Black women to a cultural genocide, and sometimes raise the specter of eugenics and population control when discussing abortion rights, as Justice Clarence Thomas of the Supreme Court did in a recent concurring opinion." The article goes on to interview a reverend and a minister, both of whom are pro-life from a religious standpoint, but remain pro-choice politically. They are in lockstep with those opposing the Alabama Human Life Protection Act: that we as a society need to provide a life where women and children can thrive, "from womb to tomb." A promise that bypasses communities of color in the US, where families are disproportionately impacted by poverty, mass incarceration, and institutionalized police brutality.

Now imagine a world where birth control is not only universally available, but exists in equal, effective measure for both sexes. And while we're here, let's expand this to envision a world where people of color no longer face the oppression and prejudice that results in racial violence and stereotyping at every turn. Where the gender a person inhabits does not impact their right to an opinion or a voice, giving all those capable of birthing (including transgender men and any applicable non-binary individuals) an equal say in how the world works. Where, on a wider level, we recognize ourselves and our sexuality as a part of nature—our thriving on par with the lives of nonhuman animals and the earth itself. In a world where all beings truly are "equal," would there be less anger and violence and self-hatred overall? Would incidences of emotional abuse and manipulation, domestic violence, and rape decrease, leading to fewer unplanned pregnancies and, ultimately, fewer abortions?

I still don't know where my decision to terminate my pregnancy fits into this picture. Although I am white and heterosexual, I am a member of an oppressed class (a woman); and yet I made a decision for a nascent life that had no voice of its own. Does this make me the oppressor? Maybe. Or maybe by making a choice for the better of my own future—one that did not result in bringing a child into a familial pattern of emotional abuse—my decision will leave the world a little bit better off.

I think about an alternate universe in which I had kept my pregnancy and found myself the mother of a person of color. It makes me recall so many small moments with the broker's family that were heart-wrenching: his seven-year-old twin nieces being teased at school for having dark hair on their faces; his ten-year-old nephew being told he wasn't allowed to wear a hoodie out of the house. But he's just a child, I said to the broker. He shrugged—this was just the way of the world. I wanted to cry, to rage against a system that threatened the safety of any child, but it didn't feel like my place. It felt like it was his grief, and I was on the outside.

Would my child have been "disadvantaged" like my friend was inclined to believe? Probably, yes. They would have faced an uphill battle in a system built to keep people of color oppressed. But just because society doesn't respect the value of a person's life, doesn't mean that value is negated. I would not have been able to protect my child from everything—no parent can. But my child would have been loved, by me and by my family. I would have done everything I could to make them know their value, as my parents did for me. In the end, this is the only shield we can offer in a world as violently oppressive to people of color as ours.

AT MY HOME IN CALIFORNIA, I have a sofa that sits in a bay window in my living room. It is my favorite reading spot—sunny in the morning, with a eucalyptus tree outside that attracts hummingbirds and fat bumblebees. After a storm, rain gathers in the gutters around my roof. If the clouds clear before the water evaporates, the reflection of the sunlight bounces in kaleidoscope patterns on the eaves of my house, just above the bay window. This is how I think of my guilt today. In the right conditions it still shows up and dances around the periphery of my mind, threatening to take a grip of my heart. But I have found ways to remind myself that my basic nature is positive and good. That what I did does not change who I am in my heart. I didn't terminate my pregnancy because I thought it was a fun thing to do with some random Monday of my life, but because I wanted to spare the world, a child, and myself, from the suffering I felt would inevitably result from me keeping it.

What I know for sure is that I still, will always, mourn the life of that child. I imagine her laughter, shining eyes and dimples. I imagine her hugs and I count her birthdays. I wish this hadn't happened to me. I wish this didn't happen to any woman, anywhere, ever. It hurts. And I think what hurts most is knowing that the fear, the shame, and the guilt of it could be softened, if we could only accept abortion as a necessary part of life as we know it in our world today. If instead of making women feel guilty and ashamed of their choice, we could focus on building a better society for tomorrow.

six

Up until I had an abortion, there had been little to regret in my life. But my body already carried one physical reminder of the scars we are left with by the regretful choices that we make. When I was 27, I pierced my ears as a birthday present to myself. I had thought about it for a few weeks, decided it was a great idea, and my then-boyfriend and I went to a hip tattooing and piercing parlor to get it done.

We waited, sitting on a cracked vinyl couch leafing through a binder with pictures of fresh tattoos, the skin pink and inflamed around the pigmented images. Towards the back of the book the pictures turned to piercings, and after a few pages we came across a picture of freshly pierced male genitalia and we slammed the book shut in a fit of giggles. This was how the piercing specialist, a burly man with a blonde ZZ Top beard and head-to-toe tattoos, found us. He was a nurse practitioner turned artist and was very soft spoken. He clearly explained the procedure as he brought me back to his chair and cleaned my lobes. He used a permanent marker to draw dots where the piercings would go. I looked in the mirror, and for the first time in my life I realized that my ears were ever so slightly uneven, which he reassured me was totally normal. The marks from the sharpie seemed centered, and I gave him the go-ahead to permanently change my, until then, unaltered body.

For the next few weeks, I was meticulous about cleaning the wounds as instructed, wiggling the gold posts back and forth, not in a screwing fashion as was the more widely used method years previously. Once the piercings were healed, I wore a pair of diamond studs that were family heirlooms, and I picked out a delicate pair of pearl earrings that dropped simply from a gold hook. For about four months, I had a love affair with my newly pierced ears.

Then I lost one of my pearl earrings at a movie that was just too loud for me, when I kept plugging my ears. It must have wiggled out. I also found that I couldn't sleep in any earrings, even some small hoops I tried out, and so I was constantly having to remember to take my earrings out before bed and put them back in first thing in the morning. When I couldn't be bothered at all, I hated the way my earlobes had a crease through them where the piercing buckled the skin.

A decision that felt so well-thought-out at the time, came to seem like the worst idea ever. I took my earrings out, the holes closed over, and now every time I see them I cringe. My ears had been pristine, smooth. The fact that they were unpierced also made me unique. My earlobes crease where the holes once were, leaving my once-perfect lobes looking like unfolded origami. I miss my unblemished earlobes. Today, I think of my scars as a good reminder about why permanent decisions, even seemingly well-thought-out ones, can so easily lead to regret.

A FULL YEAR WENT BY after my abortion. I had made the move to the coast, changed companies—though not my career—and had made good progress building a community in my new town. As the details of the abortion itself faded into memory, new thoughts and questions about *what my future could have been* began to surface in me. *How could I have not seen the light that was just up ahead? Had I have had that child, could I have made it to this good place, and raised it in a happy, healthy home for two? And maybe someday add one more?*

There was no space for these thoughts and feelings when I was still so close to the abortion. The shame, blame and guilt were so hot and loud, they crowded out everything else. Like one of Picasso's stippling paintings, I couldn't see the whole picture when I was too close to it. With some time and space, I finally began to imagine what that other life might have looked like.

What I have learned is that the decisions we make compound one another, and although many of the 35,000 choices an American makes in an average day are benign, you never know which decision may lead to regret. When I was pregnant and considering abortion I would look at my decision—to keep, or not to keep—and would try to play the tape out as far as I could for either given scenario. My mind would spin with ideas, my heart rate amping up and my body wanting to pace back and forth to burn off the energy being generated by ever more swirling thoughts. I tried to lean on past life experience, feeling into my body for what decisions had been good for me, and which I had lived to regret. In the end, I let emotion guide me; the thought of being bound to the broker for the rest of my life never once left my heart singing, and so I moved forward with my choice.

But there were blind spots in my method. When I considered parenthood, I only imagined one possible outcome, and it wasn't pretty. I never realized how much I was focused on what the worst possible scenario might look like. I never imagined that it might not be a binary choice, and that a positive co-parenting experience was just as likely as a negative one. For all the time we spend looking down the roads we might take, we'll never be able to say for certain what is in store for us.

Because the physical world we live in is painted by our thoughts and emotions, when I was depressed, isolated and anxious, the only future that I could imagine was of a bleak frozen landscape, much like Dante's Inferno: figures frigidly locked in a timeless battle with their own inner demons. My version of that was a life fraught with struggle in an unhappy co-parenting relationship, resulting in a child with low self-esteem, and an ambitious and stressful career in tech, working my way up the corporate ladder as the primary breadwinner, rather than finding a career that fulfilled me.

After I left the broker, it was amazing how quickly I was able to move on. I continued to focus on my self-care, and without the constant backwards drag of a toxic relationship, progress was all but guaranteed. I was worlds happier and found I could accomplish so much more from that headspace. From such a good place, the picture I saw when I peered back down that same path was entirely different. With a brighter outlook the fearful thoughts faded, and I knew, I just knew, that of course I could have succeeded, no matter how dark and scary a wood I may have been entering at the time. I would have made it out the other side, and I could have raised a happy, healthy child on my own.

So what do I envision now, when I think about that other path? I believe I could have found my way back to happiness, even with the broker as a co-parent. I can see the things we did agree on more clearly—the importance of education, community, and a healthy lifestyle, and the degree to which we'd want the child's grandmothers to be involved (a lot). I would still have hoped the child would spend more time with me, and maybe I'd be grateful for my few days off here and there, much like my other friends who are single parents. I could still have found a new job, begun writing, built community in a new place, and delved deeper into my own emotions to heal past hurts. These answers painted a clear picture of what my life might have looked like had I chosen that path. I can clearly see myself chasing my child around a park, tree shadows dappling the bright green grass; laughing and bonding with girlfriends while our children played with each other; and even finding a man who could love a child that was not biologically his own. When I wake up from that daydream and look around at my life without that child in it, there is a lingering feeling of regret, like a favorite misplaced ring that you can't stop checking for.

I TOLD MY CATHOLIC FRIEND about these thoughts over the phone one evening—the one who serves on the board of Planned Parenthood. Since we couldn't meet in person as often since I'd moved, we'd catch up on nights she didn't have the kids over a FaceTime dinner together.

On this night she was telling me about the point in her life where she found herself on a path similar to the one I was on with the broker. After an abortion early in her college years, she found herself pregnant again in her third year with a different boyfriend. She was devastated, fearful this would mean she would have to sacrifice her studies and ultimately her career. On the other hand, her then-boyfriend was overjoyed at the news. She was pretty far along when she found out—somewhere between 14 and 20 weeks—and for her that was past the point of no return. She was keeping that baby.

Years later she found out that her boyfriend had been cheating on her consistently with other women, and at the time of that revelation she chose to stay with him. He had always wanted another child, and they decided that growing their family might instill greater responsibility in him, and "fix" their problems. By now, our FaceTime dinner had turned into her washing dishes and me drinking my evening tea. She was shaking her head while she talked and was becoming emphatic in her speaking—clearly some frustration over the situation still lingered. She went on in her story. After years of continued infidelity, my friend found herself in the same emotional tug of war I was so familiar with: confusion, fear and helplessness on the one hand, and anger, resolve and determination on the other. It took her more than a year to work up the nerve to go, but she finally left and has been a single mom ever since.

In the seven or so years since she left that relationship behind, she has purchased a home, received her MBA, earned promotion upon promotion at work, and traveled the world. She continues to be an amazing mother to her children who, thanks to the love and stability she's provided for them as a single mom over the years, have become successful and well-adjusted children themselves. To this day they choose to spend more time with her than with her still unstable ex.

It was late by now in our call, and we'd both moved onto our couches. It almost felt like a long-distance sleepover. Her situation sounded exhausting—work, after school activities, cooking dinners, networking events, friends, and somewhere in there, dating? But it also seemed like something I'd be capable of myself. Loving a child, showing my commitment to that child day in, day out, the way my own mother always did for me, would be as natural as breathing. Even in the thick of my anxiety about the broker, concerns about money, and fear of being stuck in my job, I wonder how I could have missed the other half of this picture.

THROUGH THIS WHOLE STORY, THERE has been one figure completely missing from the picture: my father. His Alzheimer's was advanced by the time I was pregnant, and he had been living in a long-term care facility for several years. Rendered speechless by complicating factors of his disease, he is also unable to understand what I have to say. On his good days, he might give a small smile at some ribbing joke I make. But this is based on the tone of my voice, not because he recognizes my words. His disease has been his own personal war of attrition. In the early days you could see his frustration about the progress of the disease, but later he lost the cognition to recognize his decline, which might have been a blessing. My father was always the life of the party—the class clown—with a booming laugh and a huge smile. He was the first to help a friend out and was brilliant with math. He was a lifelong athlete, tall and strapping in his younger years, with broad shoulders and tan skin from so much time outside. The loss of his strength and intellect felt undignified and unfair, it made me want to scream. But watching his sense of self slip away, seeing him smile less, watching as he turned inward and no longer spoke—that was the unkindest cut of all.

My mother is my father's fourth wife. It is common knowledge in my family and has been fodder for a lot of jokes at his expense. The one where my grandma says that if he were to divorce again, they would just keep my mother in his place. There was my aunt who always told my mom that while my mother may have chosen him, the rest of us were just stuck with him. Right before their own marriage, my mom was only aware of two of his previous wives. She made a joke, *third time's the charm, right?* Only to find out that in her case, it was going to be the fourth time that needed to be the charm. She found out about the third wife only days before their wedding. Apparently two divorces didn't seem too bad to my dad, but he was afraid to mention the third, not wanting to scare off my mom. In her retelling of the story she rolled her eyes and laughed, unflappable and rock steady as always.

Not only did my dad have four wives, but he also had four children. The first, my half-brother, is 18 years older than me. I have another half-sibling, a woman, that we found out about only months before my own pregnancy. She was able to connect with our family through Facebook, reaching out to my brother and one of my dad's sisters. She had met my dad once, years before when he was well, and would eventually come to see him in his care facility when his disease was advancing. My brother—the Jesuit—and I are both the product of his final marriage to my mom. They've been married for nearly 40 years now, and she has stood faithfully by his side during all the moves, financial ups and downs, and surprises about my dad's past. In the strongest test of her love, she's been his biggest advocate and partner in this final journey of theirs. This long goodbye.

I was a daddy's girl when I was a young child. There's family lore of going to visit Santa at the mall one time and me clinging desperately to my dad's neck, wholly unwilling to let go. As I got older he was my biggest supporter in academics and sports, and as I began to make my way in the world he helped me navigate my first jobs. I don't do the best job of keeping cards and letters sent to me (another regret), so I only have one letter left from him. He wrote it shortly after my horse died—a turning point in my young life—and he had helped me find a grief counselor and an acupuncturist to help me through that difficult time, even though we were living in different cities. In the letter he talked about being lost, asking for help, and remembering that we're not alone in this world.

I wish I could talk to him and ask him about what his life looked like before I was a part of it. What made him such a sensitive man, so open with his emotions? Was there more to his story that he had never told me? Shortly after my move to California, I was home visiting him one winter morning. My mom and I had gone to visit my dad at his care facility, and we had taken him out to a west facing patio, the fence covered in vines, obscuring the less pleasing view of the parking lot beyond. We had walked slowly out to the patio, my mom supporting him by one arm, both of us assisting him into his chair. The weak winter sun was only just starting to peek over the roof of the home. I was massaging his upper back. My dad was tall, and though he'd been sick for years, his body had only just begun to lose its tone. His broad shoulders always seem so tight to me those days, and he began to hum just a little as I rubbed them. It was tuneless, a simple sound of comfort, and an expression of gratitude for one of the few small pleasures he had left. I could see his eyes, just closed, and his face relaxed. How much I wanted to ask him about what he had seen. How much I wanted to tell him about what I had been through. I would give the whole world for just one more conversation with him.

I regret that I will never have that opportunity, but if I did I would want to know the story of all four of his children: where he was when the others were born, what it felt like to have them re-enter his life at a later time. With his first wife, I imagine them walking on the college campus as she told him—she lived at home and he lived in a dorm with a roommate, so privacy would have been at a premium. It would have been nerve wracking to tell her strict, conservative father and face his anger, but honor was important to my father and he wanted to do the right thing. With his second wife, he had already left the marriage, and probably found out over the phone. My dad is an empathetic man, and I can imagine his face falling when he found out.

I wish I could tell him that when I made the decision I did, I really was doing my best. That I was trying to look out for everyone involved, the way he always looked out for me. I wish he could know what his role in my life meant to me, and that I forgave him for any of the ups and downs we did face. I'd ask him forgiveness for the ways in which I'd hurt him. Mostly, I'd want to tell him one last time how much I love him.

MY FATHER AND I DID have one conversation about abortion, and looking back I can see what a huge influence it had on me. Leading up to my sophomore year of college, I was at the bookstore buying supplies for the upcoming semester when I recognized a girl from my high school. She was very, very pregnant. Because of the sheer volume of books necessary to supply 35,000 students, there were pallets piled precariously high with books throughout the large warehouse-style room. I saw Jenny as I was nearing the registers, while she was still browsing books. She was in an enormous grey sweatshirt, belly protruding. It took me a moment to register what I was seeing. We didn't run in the same crowd in high school—I was extremely quiet and shy, whereas she was in with the popular crowd—so I didn't say hello to her. But the shock of seeing someone my age pregnant stayed with me until my next trip home, when I spoke to my father.

I mentioned before that sex and pregnancy wasn't something we spoke about in my household. But I needed to talk to my parents about it, much the same way I needed to talk to my parents two years later after I found out that a fellow high school student died during my senior year in college. Death and birth were so big and unknown to me at that point that I couldn't wrap my head around those ideas, and needed help fitting these events into the context of life. My college was about two and a half hours from my childhood home, and the distance struck a perfect balance for me: far enough to be independent, close enough to be able to get home the same day if I needed to.

That Sunday afternoon, my dad had football on the television in our garden-level living room. To this day the faint clicking of helmets and booming voice of a referee's call summons memories of afternoon naps in the sun while my dad watched his favorite teams, happily crunching Ruffles potato chips and onion dip. That day was no different. While we were watching the game, I told him about the girl I saw in the bookstore. By now it was well known that my older half-brother was very much an accident—a happy accident certainly—but unplanned nonetheless. My dad was a "floor person" and never seemed to want to use the couch. He was sitting on the beige carpet, leaned back against a coffee table under which our little terrier was fast asleep. My dad told me what it was like for him to have his first son while he was in college. At the time, he remembered feeling like he was losing his youth, and said he felt like it would be hard for Jenny too. He used that as a segue, and went on to say that he also supported a woman's right to have an abortion if she wanted. It was shocking because he came from a conservative Catholic family, and also because the topic was avoided in our household. A conversation that turned to sex or abortion would usually create an awkward silence, followed by a quick change of topic.

I wish we would have kept that conversation going and that I could have come to know more about my father. I wondered about the discussions he'd had with those women. Had they talked about abortion as an option? Did their religious beliefs keep them from considering that? Their age? Or were they just in love, and happy to have a child together? I didn't ask him those questions that day, but he made one comment that wedged itself in my mind. When he said a woman had a right to choose, he put a caveat on it: *she better do it damn quickly.*

When I was considering abortion, it was my dad's voice that

I heard whispering in the back of my mind, a grim reminder of the passage of time. I don't know how much of a role it played in the final outcome of my decision. I can only say how much urgency his assertion brought to my reality. For so many years, he was the person I turned to when I felt like my life was going off track. I wanted to hear his voice, to get a letter in his handwriting, to know he loved me, regardless of my choices in this—the most moral decision of my life. He won't know how powerful his words were to me. As my life coach says, *the world can turn on a dime with a perfectly placed pearl of wisdom.* That may have been an offhand comment, but it will stay with me for the rest of my life.

This story came back to me during that visit to Arizona, the one where I sat with my dad in the milky morning sunlight. Why had that been his counsel when I came to him with the story of my young friend being pregnant? Did it have to do with him having two unplanned children of his own, or was there more to his story that I didn't know? What did he regret? Missed time with his older children, the pain he caused some of his ex-wives, time away from my brother and I when we were young and he had to travel for his job managing large sales accounts? These things I know about, but I'll always be left to wonder if my story was his story as well, and if this was why he mentioned abortion that long-ago Sunday morning.

WE LIVE IN AN AGE where we have so much choice in life, particularly in developed nations. We have access to food from around the world in any season, education that opens doors to every career we can dream up, and technology now allows us to be digital nomads— choosing where and when we work. As amazing as this is, such a boundless array of choice can leave us paralyzed in the face of life-changing decisions, and full of anxiety that we may be missing out on what we didn't choose.

In this world, the idea of a life lived with no regret seems to me old-fashioned and romantic. Regret is inherent in life and is even more prevalent in a life of choice. My father lived with the pain of missing decades of his son and daughter's lives, but in the end he found his way back to them, and loved them. With my half-brother, my dad got to be a doting grandfather, and became friends with his adult son. They traveled to see one another and enjoyed long meals and fun adventures. My friend regrets staying in her own bad relationship for so long when there were so many other opportunities available to her in life, but she loves her children to the depths of her soul.

During my research for this book I found an essay by Caitlin McDonnell, whose experience had so many similarities to my own that I'd be remiss not to include her words here. Her essay is titled "The Abortion I Didn't Want," which could easily have been a title for this book. She says, "If I had remained pregnant, I'd have been bringing into the world a child with a dearth of stability and a father who'd stated clearly that he didn't want him. I think I probably would have made it work somehow, but my wanting a child at that point was not compatible with the reality of my circumstances and it would have tied me irrevocably to a man I didn't trust." Ultimately, I made the same choice for the same reasons, and have dealt with the same complex emotions she details in her writing. I regret the life I have missed out on because of the baby I didn't have, but am building a new life, full of opportunity and wonder. Which is to say, regret doesn't always mean that we are doing the wrong things. Maybe there is no "right" path, just a different one.

seven

~

I've moved a lot in my life, and when I first arrived in California I leaned into my past experience of making new homes in new places. I know that it takes a while to find all your favorites: be it coffee shops, trails, or friend groups. You have to go into things with an open mind, be patient, and remain persistent. Though I had found some great running buddies right off the bat, I didn't yet have anyone here I felt like I could really confide in, so I relied on friends from my past when things felt a little rocky. During any move there will inevitably be some tough patches—usually a few months in when the solo exploring is getting old but you don't quite have your new routine nailed down.

About four months after my move I was having a restless weekend and a hard time getting a hold of my old friends. I finally settled on sending a video message in lieu of a live call with someone, and after lamenting that I hadn't made friends here (yet!) I somehow wound up going down the path of: *if I'd kept that pregnancy, I wouldn't be so lonely.* Selfish, but true. I found myself choked up to the point where I had to put down my phone. As I was curled over myself quietly crying, I flashed on a memory—the kind that reaches out to you through your senses.

My first encounter with the concept of physical memory was as a little girl, watching it happen to my mom after her father passed away. She was reaching for something in our guest closet without knowing one of her dad's Pendleton shirts was hanging there. The smell of the shirt wafted to her face—his particular scent, fresh starch and a hot iron—and immediately drew her to his memory. She stopped what she was doing, and as though in a trance she reverently took his shirt out of the closet, sat gently on the bed, and closed her eyes as she buried her face in the cloth and took a deep breath. Something so tangible brought her right back to his side.

My flesh memory now was of myself, years ago, after another move, curled over myself in the same pose, crying. Just before I turned 30, my life turned into a series of losses. I had been living on the East Coast for about nine months with my boyfriend of nearly six years—we'd left Colorado when he received a promotion at his job that required him to work from corporate HQ. My dad's health had been declining for a couple of years at this point, but we still didn't know for sure what was going on with him.

Beginning in August of that year, things began to crumble: my dad was given his final (and terminal) diagnosis, and I left that boyfriend and moved back across the country, where I felt like I belonged. Though we'd been together for so long, it was the uncertainty of our future that led to our breakup. I wanted to marry and have children; he wasn't there yet and wasn't sure when he'd get there. We'd both bent as far as we could to make things work, but finally the relationship broke. When I arrived back in Colorado, the town was in the midst of a hundred-year flood. Canyon roads were completely washed out, landslides reshaped the foothills, and our normally quiet creeks turned into machines of death: full of debris, the color of Hershey's syrup, and with so much water that house-sized boulders were tossed around like pebbles. The flood claimed lives, and quite literally wiped parts of the town off the map.

Then, while prepping my beloved dog for knee surgery, we discovered she had a kidney disease. She stayed healthy for a few months, but subsequently went into a quick decline. As the disease took her appetite, she began to drop weight and lose energy. There were some palliative care measures we took, but ultimately it was an incurable disease. She had been my baby, my closest companion, and favorite adventure buddy for eight years. Saying goodbye to her was the hardest day of my life. Arriving home from the vet's office that day was surreal; I hadn't yet come to terms with the fact that she was gone. I felt hollowed out, as though watching her leave me eroded the core of my being, leaving a gaping hole from my throat to the pit of my stomach.

Up until this point, my life had been so carefree. That was the word I always used: *carefree*. Before moving to the East Coast, my boyfriend and I had mountain-biked together, traveled together, hiked with our dog together. I had strong, outdoorsy girlfriends, and we spent weekends backpacking, camping and biking in the Rocky Mountains. We got as far away from civilization as we could, to marvel at the scenery and coo over wildlife. In the backcountry I felt alive, as though I could really breathe and stretch my legs. Looking up at the stars gave me a sense of awe and wonder—the size of the universe is unfathomable to me, and it brings home my gratitude for my very life. It was on these trips that I developed a deep love and respect for nature. I loved seeing the interconnectedness of all things, and marveled at the beauty and perfection in the balance of life. Faith is not something that comes easily to me, but I feel most connected to the divine when I'm in nature, and I reveled in spending time in its presence. I could leave for these adventures without a worry: my parents were, for the most part, healthy. My career wasn't quite where I wanted it, sure, but that was another problem for another day. Life was good and it seemed as through the sun was always shining.

Then, like the flood that ravaged my town, wave after wave of disaster rolled into my life. While I was in it, I was just doing my best to keep my head above water. But looking back, this period of my life felt like the end of my innocence. I realized everyone I loved wasn't going to live forever, and that life wasn't an endless stream of powder days conquered by bodies young and strong, happy relationships, and blue-skied beachy vacations.

There are so many vivid scenes that paint a picture of that time in my memory. My dad, his dementia having robbed him of the ability to gently articulate hard truths, telling me about my dog's condition straight over the phone: *she is dying.* Watching my parents getting off a plane and for the first time ever thinking, *they look old.* Being on my knees next to my best friend's guest bed, holding myself as hard as I could because I had so much love for this man who had been my future, and suddenly I had nowhere to put that love. It was such a depressive, trying time in my life—I wasn't sleeping well, and even "normal" life decisions seemed to take all of my energy. The sun had disappeared behind a heavy, dark cloud.

I had been brought to my knees, and I knew I needed help navigating this new territory. I found a grief counselor, a lovely woman in her 50s who was a grad of the local liberal arts college, Naropa, which had been founded by a Tibetan Buddhist teacher. Her philosophy on grief was rooted in impermanence, and that we suffer when we fail to accept or acknowledge that fact. If we can realize and allow changes— to what is in our lives, and to the core of who we believe we are—we can feel the pain of loss without being stuck in a cycle of suffering. She practiced art therapy, and though I found it a bit "woo-woo" at the time, it carried me through those dark days. Her office was in a brick building that overlooked a nursery school and neighboring park, and we could often hear children outside during our sessions. In her muted blue office, I created mandalas with shimmering watercolors, putting all my emotions into the paint on the page, as we slowly paid reverence to everything I loved that I now found myself saying good-bye to. We pried open the idea that not only did I need to grieve the loss of my dog and my dad as I knew him, but I also needed to grieve the person I had been. This meant saying goodbye to the carefree girl I loved so much, while stepping into a new role as a veteran of life. I shifted from drifting on the winds of fortune, to actively steering my life—something I had always tried to do, without ever quite succeeding. I had made significant decisions on my own, and was proud of myself for it: I had left a relationship with no future, I had given my companion the best quality of life I could for as long as seemed moral, and I had begun to face the reality of my dad's disease head on, helping my mom and my brother navigate this as equals.

Spending a season of life brought to my lowest, and seeing myself through that time, I no longer took for granted the good things life brought my way. Instead, a new, and tangible, understanding of impermanence made me grateful for what I had, in the same way that a traveler doesn't realize the comforts of home until they've left.

AS IT IS WITH LIFE, there were more good days ahead. After I adjusted to being single and without a dog, I got a job in management at a company that felt out of my league. I excelled under the pressure of having harder problems to solve, and I learned from and led my coworkers through my first major project. I traveled the world, learning Spanish as I explored Central and South America with a new boyfriend. Eventually I fell in love again, much to my surprise, and was giddy like a schoolgirl. I caught myself smiling and laughing as I twirled down the street, too happy to keep it all inside. I learned the meaning of the expression *day by day* when dealing with my father's illness. When I saw him, we worked with what he could do that visit, and upon leaving, I knew I'd have to recalibrate my expectations for the next trip. This day-by-day acceptance of his illness let me appreciate the time we still had together. I felt as though I had passed the test, and life was rewarding patience and groundedness with financial stability, happiness, and new opportunities.

Life continued on this mostly even keel for several more years. There were some changes, sure—I moved to Arizona to take care of my ailing father and left a relationship and a job during the move. But they all seemed like *good* changes, necessary at that point in my life. By all measures, my life was heading in a good direction. Until one day I looked up, and realized I had wandered off the path and was once again lost in the woods. As Ernest Hemingway once said about bankruptcy, it happened "gradually, then suddenly." For a time, my career path felt fulfilling, but it slowly became more bureaucratic. By then, I was dating the broker, and that was rocky but passable until the abortion, and my uncovering of his porn addiction and infidelity. Arizona had a lot to offer, but I still found the city oppressive. If there is a rock bottom in my story, it was actually after the abortion. I knew how bad things were, I tried to leave, and I wound up going back to him.

As things started to go south again, I grappled again with impermanence, and with the vision I had of myself. I had lived by the code: do good and be good, remain kind and compassionate, and life will be kind to you. I kept a budget and paid my taxes on time. I took care of my ailing dad. I went to church with my mom from time to time. I was a vegan. I volunteered downtown at a shelter feeding women and children who faced food insecurity. Even though I'd had an abortion, I still identified as a "good girl" and good girls should be happy. I beat myself up for feeling stuck. At the time, I couldn't recognize the impermanence of those emotions: that good days would come and go throughout the duration of my life.

I also missed the truth that as our perspective changes, things don't seem so black and white. Periods of our life that may have felt difficult, will later look simple. It is like the Taoist parable of the Chinese farmer. One day, a poor Chinese farmer's best horse runs away. The townspeople say, "How horrible!" But the farmer replies, "Good, bad, who knows." Shortly thereafter the horse returns, with a magnificent stallion in tow. The townspeople are amazed at his fortune. The farmer again replies, "Good, bad, who knows." The parable continues: his son breaks a leg taming the horse, but because of the break he misses a draft for a deadly war. *Good, bad, who knows.* Our lives are a journey. Our experiences will look different six days, six months, six years from now. Labeling everything we do, who we think we are, and what we think our futures should look like, keeps us stuck in a cycle seeking permanence, leaving us dispirited when once again it's swept away from us.

I keep a copy of Dante's *Divine Comedy* on my bookshelf. The great Florentine's masterpiece opens with the lines, "Midway upon the journey of our life/I found myself within a forest dark/For the straightforward pathway had been lost." Those words brought me back to my therapist's office from so many years ago, explaining to her that I had lost my way, that the trail that had once seemed so clear was now overgrown. I was again wrestling with my sense of self, I had endured losses, I didn't know where to go with my life.

I know now that these seasons come and go. As we move through life, we can look at a period of grief as nothing greater than loss and sadness. Or we can turn it into an opportunity to shed the skin of who we once were and become more tender versions of ourselves: more empathetic, compassionate, and understanding of where people are coming from. Processing grief is necessary to move forward in life. And grief is an emotion that goes so far beyond losing a loved one. In any transitory time in our lives, we move through a period of saying goodbye, changing, moving forward. The difference with abortion is that there is no playbook for this particular kind of grief. We're left alone, on that dark and overgrown path, with no way to name what we are feeling.

IN THE US, 70% OF abortions are performed at free-standing clinics, rather than at the offices of gynecologists and primary care physicians. The number of clinics per state varies directly with the political stance of the state legislature. In conservative states this means the few (and sometimes only) clinic(s) available are situated in large cities. For the vast majority of women receiving abortions in our country, this means treatment is out of step with the rest of the gynecological care they receive throughout their lives.

For me, specifically, this meant that when my emotions went haywire after my abortion, I assumed it was all due to the ambivalence and complexity of my decision-making process. In the fog of grief (and gynecological care not being my area of expertise), I never considered that it could be due to a massive shift in my hormones. I received wonderful care at the clinic where I was seen, but this small but important fact was somehow overlooked, or not stressed enough. I can't help but think that with more continuous care—like through my standard gynecologist's office, for example—this non-trivial detail may have been noted in some additional follow-up or phone call.

I had physical symptoms too. In the days after the abortion, my sleep cycles were disrupted; I woke sometime close to four a.m., was exhausted by nine a.m., and then got my energy back again after lunch. That eased pretty quickly, but symptoms of a disrupted appetite and general brain fog lasted for much longer. For weeks, I was generally nauseated and rarely hungry. It wasn't until I had to roll the waistband of my jeans under to keep them up that I realized how much weight I had lost. My focus at work was a dim and distant memory. I felt forgetful and distracted, my mind wandering off in meetings. I often had to scramble on Sundays to catch up on work I didn't do during the week. I didn't recognize these as symptoms of grief, because they were so different from the general depression I felt the first time I went through a series of losses.

Not to mention, there is no expectation and no instructions for women on how to mourn the loss of a child to abortion. We're supposed to just deal with our feelings along with the physical fallout. Funerals usually serve as an opportunity for us to share our grief with our loved ones, and express our thoughts and emotions within the framework of our faith. But there is no funeral for an abortion, and any ceremony we may need to process what we're feeling is expected to happen quietly and alone, ideally without making a mess, or spewing our emotions on anyone who happens to come too close.

I dealt with it by spending more time in my car, always my car, crying alone, usually into my scarf, often in between meetings. I just had no other space to be alone with my feelings. My office was made of glass; I jokingly called it the fishbowl. I certainly couldn't go to a priest, and the broker didn't want me crying at home. It came up more than once and was the subject of what I considered our worst fight ever, though he remembers it differently. One evening on the way home from work I stopped by my mom's house to visit and pass time—the broker was going to be home late that evening and I didn't want to wait for him at the house alone. I texted him to verify that I should head home at the time we had planned on. I didn't hear back, so I called. He exploded, yelling at me through the phone that I was too emotional and needy, something I had never experienced before or after. It shut me up there and then. I no longer showed vulnerability at home; I put away my tears and sadness and developed a hard outer shell. I see pictures of myself from that time, and aside from being a little skinnier, I don't look all that different. What stands out to me is how few pictures there were, how few things I had to celebrate or remember. I had locked myself away.

This has turned out to be a theme, repeated among the women I know who have also been through this. My dear friend Julie, the one I told about my abortion in her kitchen, my hands shaking as I sliced lettuce for our salad, had a similar experience. The day of her abortion, which she had done as an outpatient procedure, she came home feeling crampy, sad, and vulnerable. They were living in one of the first apartments they had together, and it was small and clean, but without any frills, filled with hand-me-down furniture courtesy of their parents. Soup sounded like it would be a comfort for her body, and the idea of giving herself this gentle nourishment warmed her heart. She microwaved her brothy chicken noodle soup and walked to the table, past her husband, who had been with her for the procedure. He was on the phone in the kitchen. This was before the days of cell phones, Julie reminded me, so he was tethered to the wall on a landline with a curly cord. As she set her soup down, the scalding liquid sloshed and landed on her lap. Having been on the verge of tears all day, her eyes began to overflow, and she looked to her husband for support. He saw the mess and turned away, finalizing golf plans with some buddies for the weekend. It was her body, her choice, and her grief to process. She would be alone on her journey through that dark emotional landscape, looking for resolution, finding her way to the other side.

The negative associations with abortion keep us from feeling safe and secure in being vulnerable and talking to other women. I myself have been caught in the trap of stereotyping who is or isn't the "type of woman" who has had an abortion, or who may or may not be accepting of my decision. Henri Nouwen, a Jesuit psychologist whose work my brother introduced me to, coined the term "Wounded Healer" to describe people who, having been wounded themselves, seek to heal others who are going through the same experience. In fact, a British researcher, Alison Barr, has shown that 74 percent of counselors and psychotherapists have faced "wounding experiences" themselves. In our own way, each of us who shares our stories of struggle, grief and pain embodies this Wounded Healer archetype. With no societal ceremonies to mark the event of an abortion, such as funerals or open periods of grieving, we can only lean on each other to help find our way through these complex feelings and emotionally charged landscapes.

THE 2015 DISNEY PIXAR FILM *Inside Out* tells the story of emotions through the life of a young girl, and shows us how sadness can be pushed to the side in favor of other, more positive emotions. In the movie we go inside the head of young Riley and meet each of her emotions, named Joy, Anger, Fear, Disgust and Sadness. After first ostracizing Riley, and then sending her on an emotional rollercoaster, Sadness finally proves her value by the end of the film. She is the emotion that helps Riley connect to her parents, by sharing her sorrow at having moved away from her first home. Sadness acts as an alarm bell, telling the young girl when she needed help.

Psychology researcher Joseph Forgas explains that grief (one form of sadness) lasts longer than emotions like fear and anger by a significant degree—where fear and anger may last for minutes, sadness lasts for days. The value of fear and anger have long been understood from an evolutionary standpoint. Fear triggers the flight response in humans: when something startles you, you jump. Anger causes the fight response. When a friend says something (heaven forbid the truth) that stings, the instinct is to hit back, even though striking back at the people we love rarely works to our benefit. The purpose of grief and its manifestations—the turning inward, intense sorrow, numbness, bitterness, lack of joy—has taken more time to suss out.

But Forgas' research is beginning to uncover the meaning and purpose of grief. It has been shown that sadness improves memory and judgment, and that people become more generous when sad. They are more likely to address and change whatever situation caused their sadness than they would be if the situation were fueled by anger or fear. Understandable, since anger is so fleeting and sadness is so lasting. People who are in a sad state tend to be much more sensitive to social norms. We see it all the time when families set aside past hurts and grudges when they attend a funeral. The pain that accompanies grief, and the depth of our love for the person who passed on, is stronger than the anger or discord that may exist between us.

Grief and sadness also benefit us on a larger, societal scale, by uniting us in that shared emotional experience. The greater the loss and the deeper the sadness, the more a community knits together and helps each other out in whatever way they can. There is no clearer example of this than what occurred in the United States in the days following 9/11. The fall of the towers came soon after the 2000 presidential election, when Gore lost because of our electoral college, and a couple of pesky hanging chads. More than half of our country felt cheated and angry, and as a country we couldn't have been more divided (or so we thought, until 2020 came along). I was able to be with my family shortly after the attack started, and from my childhood home we watched planes crash and buildings tumble on TV. I had never before experienced pain and grief on such an immense scale. As a nation, we set down our differences without hesitation and came together, our sadness acting as an emotional signal that we needed each other's help.

Grief and sadness can also generate great purpose in our lives, motivating us to take action. Some take up the mantle of a worthy cause or carry on the legacy of a loved one. Others realize more deeply that life is short and precious, and leverage this newfound understanding as motivation to pursue their calling. We can and do use our grief to spur us on. Sisters and daughters run 5Ks in memory of an aunt lost to breast cancer, donations pour into research foundations after the loss of a spouse to cystic fibrosis. This happens not only when loved ones pass, but even when the threat of loss is on the horizon. When our friends and family are afflicted, we can move mountains.

In this way, grief becomes more than an emotional response to tragedy and loss; it becomes a catalyst for change and a source of motivation, wielded to honor what we're grieving—whether it is a part of who we once were, a person, or even a belief. Grief channeled into action becomes an outlet, and a way to move forward without forgetting.

I lost a cousin when I was 27. He overdosed on drugs, though my aunt and uncle thought that foul play might have been involved. Charlie was 20 at the time, and though I'm not close with many of my cousins, we had spent a good amount of our formative years together. We were all devastated when he passed, his immediate family in particular. His funeral was enormous—filled with family, friends, and so many members of the community—something all too common at funerals of the young. For my aunt, the pain just never seemed to end. It's now been nine years since he died, but if you were speaking to her, you'd think he was still alive today. *Oh, Charlie just loved gingersnaps! You know, Charlie donated 24 pints of blood in his lifetime?* That's three gallons! She wears her grief on the outside, but has used it to change many lives by taking up the cause of blood donation that he left behind. Her, my uncle, and my two other cousins donate blood every 56 days, rain or shine. By remembering him so actively, she gets to live with the son she won't see again in this earthly life and also make a tangible impact on this world.

Zooming out again, we see how the Black Lives Matter movement was born out of societal grief. BLM began in 2013 in the wake of the acquittal of Trayvon Martin's murderer. Since its inception, the organization has been involved in countless methods of action for social justice, becoming the global emblem of my generation's civil rights movement. All of this born from the grief of Black lives lost to violence.

Turning grief into action is less clear when the loss is a silent one, like in the case of the countless Black people's lives to racism in the United States before there was a movement to *say their names.* Like with abortion and miscarriage, too. When Laila asked me once if I had mourned this baby, I wasn't quite sure how to answer her. My child had no name. And though some people have the remains of their fetus cremated, my abortion was so early that there were quite literally no remains to collect. At the time of my abortion I was still with the broker, and dealing with so much turmoil that the idea of a ritual of some nature never even crossed my mind. Looking back at it now, I know that my emotions were so walled up when I was around him that it would have been hard for me to unwind enough to have a ceremony even when I was alone.

So where does this leave us when we're supposed to hide our grief away? Crying in my car acted as a physical release valve when I needed it most, and in that way it was important to my healing. Crying eased the negative emotions, but also made me feel close to the child I had lost—as though it was a space we shared together. Even though

I had found a good space to process, I felt isolated. I had no work or cause to channel it into at that point, and initially, not a lot of people to share my experience with. So it festered, unmoving, a trapped ball of slow, agitating energy in the pit of my stomach.

NEAR THE END OF OUR relationship I did finally get some closure, and although I can't say for sure, I think the broker did too. On our last trip together, though we didn't know at the time that it would be, the broker finally asked me about the abortion. Traffic was bad coming out of the city that day, so we got a later start than we had hoped. By the time we were coming through the San Bernardino Mountains it was dark, and the winding roads felt dodgy. I was driving and was being blinded by headlights around every hairpin turn. In my exhausted state the road felt downright dangerous, and the tension of concentrating had given me a headache.

Until, out of nowhere, the broker broke the monotony of dashed lines and the hum of tires with a soft statement, *You haven't talked about the abortion at all lately.* He caught me off guard and it felt like one more twist to the knife in my stomach, which was already clenched with anxiety. It was a taboo topic in our house, and we hadn't spoken about it in over a month. But I could tell by his tone that he wasn't looking for a fight. I recounted to him, in my own gentle manner, his pleas for me to keep my tears out of the house. From the passenger seat, he tucked some wayward hairs behind my right ear. It was a tender gesture, and I could tell he was selecting his next words carefully. I *didn't need you to stop talking about it entirely. It was just the constant crying. It was too much. I was trying to process things in my own way, and your emotions were overwhelming. There wasn't any room for my feelings.* I could see what he meant. Right after the abortion I had lived my grief out loud, until all at once I fell silent. I had turned my grief inward and become a ghost. Now, he was sharing that from his vantage point, he had taken this as a signal that I had stopped caring. I told him that couldn't be further from the truth. The past months had been so, so hard for me. *Me too*, he echoed.

My gas light turned on and I was tearing up a bit. I thought it best to pull over. I glanced over and found that he was crying too. We pulled into a deserted gas station, fluorescent lights blazing in a sea of darkness. A bent chain-link fence barely held back brush from the undeveloped hillside beyond the parking lot. From that unexpected place, we grieved together for the first time. We held each other, recognizing aloud our distinct responsibilities in what had happened. I apologized for the pain I must have caused by needing so much of him at first, and then blocking him out when he couldn't handle my emotions. I also recognized how hard it must have been to feel like he had no control for the duration of my pregnancy. In turn, he apologized for the back and forth he caused, and for his anger when I was at my lowest.

We went on to acknowledge that no matter how many other children we might someday have, that pregnancy would always be our first. I told him about my deep regret and the constant undercurrent of guilt I felt. He admitted that he had similar feelings and that he carried a strong sense of loss.

My tears eventually morphed into hiccups and the broker ran inside to get some water and snacks for the next day. He took over driving to give me a break. We were mostly silent for the remainder of the drive, both wiped out from the emotional outpouring. But something healed in me that night. I was on the path to leaving our relationship by then, but was allowing myself the time and space I needed to do it. That moment of shared grief released me from the need to create a family with him to make up for what we had done. In the space of an outbreath, the weight of a thousand pounds lifted off my shoulders, and months of tension left my body. By naming that child's place in our personal histories, and in our family, I knew I could move on.

When I recognize grief in myself today, be it about the abortion, the slow loss of my dad, or any of the other losses I have accumulated along the way, I take the time to feel into it, recognizing that the depth of my grief is a good barometer of the profundity of my love. But I have also found ways to channel that grief into action, in writing this book, or even just writing in my journal. And when it feels appropriate, I reach out to others who share my experience. Writing and conversation—the story medicine I've written about previously—has been a way for humans to process grief since the dawn of language. Opening ourselves to another person's experience not only shares the burden of grief, but gives us the opportunity to look at our own journey through a new lens, shifting our perspective from judgment to curiosity, from pain to growth.

eight

~

Once, years before my move to California, I was visiting San Diego with a group of swimmer friends when a routine day in the ocean turned into the scariest experience I've had in open water. Though the swim was short, the overwhelming strength of the ocean reminded me of the precariousness and fragility of my life—leading to an over- whelming sense of gratitude and relief getting back on dry land. Not a jumping around with glee joy, but a *fall to the ground weeping* for the fact that I was still alive.

That morning, my friends and I played round after round of beach volleyball (we were all terrible) and had walked up and down the boardwalk eating mangoes on a stick. Once we were all good and cooked by the sun, we decided it was time for a dip.

Earlier, "No Swimming" signs had been posted on the beach due to a high surf advisory. The waves weren't big, but they looked rough. Instead of breaking slowly from one side to another, they slammed shut all at once, creating a great booming sound as water exploded into foam. As the day wore on the waves had become noticeably more mellow, and the guards pulled the signs. Before getting in we watched some surfers for a few minutes to see how quickly the longshore cur- rent was moving. They were sitting up on their boards, clad in full body wetsuits chatting and glancing over their shoulders looking for the next set. As a group, they appeared to be approaching the pier (the only fixed location we could see) at a reasonably slow rate. They wouldn't have been out at all if the waves were still slamming shut, and we deemed it safe to get in.

We made our way past the breakers at an easy pace. I was taking long strokes and could feel the cold water slipping past on my torso and legs. My breathing was calm and rhythmic, and I popped my head up from time to time to sight off the pier and see where my friends were. The sun was directly overhead, making the light nearly blinding, and rendering the normally cerulean blue water sepia-toned and flat. The water was murky from the choppy surf earlier in the day.

I was relaxed, trying to keep my focus on my stroke and my thoughts away from what might be swimming just a few feet below me, undetected. The pace was easy, and we broke a couple of times to regroup. After one stop, we realized that the current was pulling us faster than we'd anticipated and decided it was best to head to shore now to avoid getting tangled up in the pier, where the water would become choppy and confused—its wooden pilings crusted with razor sharp barnacles that could rip a swimmer to shreds.

We turned east to shore and made quick work reaching the breakers. Immediately when we hit the surf, the group broke apart. We raised no alarm; we knew we could all make it in and the last thing we wanted was for the lifeguards to risk themselves rescuing us. But it was a long, hard, scary swim in. The pattern was simple: I'd swim forward a few feet only to see the next wave bearing down on me. I'd dive to avoid taking a wave on the head and would swim so deep that it would start to get dark. Once the wave rolled by overhead, I'd pop back up, get a few gulps of air, swim forward, and the whole thing would begin again. The pier and its barnacled pilings were growing menacingly closer all the while.

I finally made it in, only yards from the pier. Lifeguards were waiting at the water's edge to check on me, and to remind me of the danger I'd put myself in. I felt chastised, embarrassed, and thoroughly humbled. I know the power of water, understand the danger of underestimating its strength, and yet somehow my friends and I had misjudged the conditions and made a rookie mistake.

I cried that night before bed. The swim had exhausted me and completely burnt my adrenals out, and although I felt safe once I was ashore, it wasn't until I was fed, sheltered, and tucked under the covers that my body felt safe enough to release the pent-up anxiety of the day. My limbs relaxed, something in my stomach unwound itself, and my shoulders finally dropped from around my ears. I cried because I had been so scared. But I also cried because I knew that I would wake up in the morning, and there were people around the world who wouldn't. I cried because I was so, so lucky. I slept like a rock.

The following morning, I got up late, and went down to the beach with the sun already up, where I took myself out to a Mexican-food brunch and drank two cups of strong coffee. It was a cloudless day, and the beach was peaceful, populated only by some morning walkers. The feeling in my body was of sunshine radiating from my soul, as surely as it had burst over the eastern horizon. I felt so alive, and so grateful to have another day ahead of me.

That was years ago, but still well into the era of *gratitude as an attitude* being mainstream. I'd hopped fully on the bandwagon, and practiced writing lists of things I was grateful for and putting them in a big jar, giving thanks for all the blessings in my life before bed, and weaving the concept of gratitude into my daily meditations. I was making an effort, but looking back now, that all feels so shallow. Swaths of my day would still zoom past me, unnoticed, as I tried to pinpoint the "good things" that happened in my life. It's been experiences like that swim, and the abortion, that have helped me to remember that I am grateful to be alive, each and every day.

ALTHOUGH MY CLOSE SHAVE IN THE OCEAN WAS NOT EXACTLY a near-death experience, I came out of it refreshed, awake to all that my life had to offer—and that shift has never been more essential to me than it is right now. I am writing this chapter in late March of 2020 and the state of California is going into its second week of a stay-at-home order to slow the spread of COVID-19. It is a scary, uncertain time. Sitting at my kitchen table, watching the sunset paint the distant mountains pink, the news feed on my phone brings in a sea of scary information: disease modeling of expected death toll by country; economic projections of how long and deep of a groove COVID might carve into our financial landscape; nursing home residents being wiped out, wholesale, like the shelves in our grocery stores.

Buried among these stories, a few headlines catch my eye—those mentioning states attempting to restrict abortion access during the pandemic, the argument being that abortions are a nonessential medical service. All masks and gowns, which our country is currently short on, should be redirected to hospitals treating coronavirus patients. I sigh as I read this, unhappy but unsurprised.

We don't know, but can only assume, that during a time of lockdown unintended pregnancies (and domestic abuse) may be on the rise. With three out of four of us confined to our homes, and many women without consistent access to birth control, I imagine at least some will soon be checking their fertility apps just like I did, realizing they've missed a period, and wondering what to do next. Taking myself back to the day I found out I was pregnant, and playing out what that scenario would look like today, I can practically feel my heart beginning to race. *Oh, please. Not me. Not now.* Finding out that you're accidentally pregnant is a lot to deal with at the best of times, let alone with the added burden of trying to find access to a procedure with so many clinics shut down. For women who are able to access the care they need, there is also the added worry of contracting the virus.

At the time of my abortion, I knew it was a privilege to be able to take time off work to seek medical care—to not have to leave my city to have a doctor's visit, and to be able to take the pills in the comfort and privacy of my own home. I was also in a position where I could pay for any procedure or medication that I needed. Today, I realize how fortunate I was that this happened to me under "normal" circumstances. Though I lived in a generally red state at the time, Arizona, and despite the growing conservatism under the Trump administration, access was still available and made relatively easy.

Reading these frightening new headlines makes it hard to stay present, to remember that, for today, my family is safe, and that we'll deal with whatever tomorrow brings when it arrives. By any measure—global or local—my stay-at-home situation would fall into the category of "above average." I am safe, I am not alone, and I am able to work from my kitchen table.

Pandemics are nothing new to humanity, but this is a first for my generation, and that of any of my living relatives. As an upper-middle class white woman living in America today, the current situation really drives home how much I take my freedom for granted. The interruption of our lives as we know it has only further highlighted the many ways that I am fortunate. In America, most of us have near constant access to clean, running water with which to wash our hands. Most of us live in temperature-controlled homes, and we can obtain food easily, whether through stores or food banks. And although it is currently overwhelmed, and is certainly imperfect, we have a healthcare system that functions, and that the majority have access to. Even while at home full-time, I am able to stay connected to my friends and family thanks to technology. I can cook healthy meals and I still participate with my exercise community, keeping up with our workouts via the internet. In comparison to a developing nation, or worse, a refugee camp, we live like kings and queens. It makes me sad to the point of tears that not everyone is as safe as me.

Back in my kitchen, the sun has gone down and my tea has gone cold. I've spent the better part of a few hours sieving through my news feed. I wonder how many women will wake tomorrow scared and isolated, facing the challenge of an unwanted pregnancy. I put my teacup in the sink and start chopping some vegetables for soup, letting my mind wander as I go through the motions of making a meal. Privilege gives us so many things to be grateful for. And so often, privilege comes down to nothing more than luck.

ONE OF THE ARTICLES I found myself reading that afternoon was a particularly well written essay examining the myriad difficult choices that lie ahead of us as we move through the pandemic. One of the questions put forward by the author was whether we would be willing, as a people, to hand over the keys to our bodies in exchange for greater safety from the virus. Would we be okay with mandatory quarantine with no option to see our loved ones, as they are doing in China? What about having our location monitored and to allow an app to trace our contacts? Or compulsory health checks and vaccines? Sovereignty over our own bodies is something people have fought long and hard for, over centuries, and these suggestions trigger yet more realizations about how anti-abortion laws want to take that away from women.

Perhaps because I have taken for granted that abortion is legal in my country, until now I have never been particularly passionate about the argument that abortion seeks to control women's bodies. But imagining a future where we no longer have physical autonomy due to the coronavirus shook something loose in me, and I was finally able to imagine what it would feel like to be controlled in that way. Wearing a mask is one thing, but picturing myself being forced to have a health check, I arrived at a visceral understanding of the fact that the government should have no say in what I do with my body: where I choose to live, the medical practices I feel are right for me, and whether or not I choose to bear a child. But where do we draw that line? In a pandemic, wearing masks to save countless lives seems obvious (to me, at least), but at what point does the policing of our bodies become coercive control? Further, who should be answering these questions—individuals, or governments?

I find the framework around abortion today to be reductionist and one-dimensional, focused almost entirely on the question surrounding whose body we're considering—a woman's right to choose vs. the rights of an unborn fetus. This school of thought leaves out everything that cannot be counted or measured. We don't consider things like the value of a woman's emotional well-being, or her hopes and dreams for her future; be it pursuing her career, or starting a different family under better circumstances. We don't think about her culture, her family system, or her religious counsel, and how these things may impact her choice, or how they may or may not support her after the fact. We don't consider the wider societal impact of our government sending a message to women that says, *you don't know what is best for your own body*. And, by extension, *your own life*. Every woman is a unique grouping of these attributes, and every woman's life brings different value to the world. To force a woman to have a child she doesn't want denounces that value and keeps her from the fullest expression of herself. And although this is definitely a "women's" issue, I try to remember that it impacts the men in this world as well.

Soon after I moved to California, on the day I moved from my motel into my top-floor sublet, I met a guy. Having only a handful of boxes made the move easy, but it was a hot day and I had to navigate two sets of stairs to get everything in. By the time I was done, I was sweaty, dusty, and not exactly looking my best. I was also hungry. I wandered down to a street known for a strip of restaurants and stopped into the first taco shop I saw. Within moments of ordering, Blake came over and struck up a conversation about my Colorado t-shirt. Easy going and kind, right off the bat, he was the quintessential blonde-haired, blue-eyed California boy.

We exchanged numbers, went for a hike, and before I knew it, we were spending every weekend together. I could see the danger in this: I was new in town, and if we spent all our time together but it didn't work out, I'd be left with a gaping hole in my social calendar. But it was easy, and fun, and felt like such a lighthearted way to get to know my way around. He was outdoorsy, like me, and he introduced me to many local hiking and running trails. We'd wander the main street together with no agenda, popping our heads in different shops and eventually land on a dinner spot. On one such lazy Saturday we were sprawled across my bed in the sun, windows open to a cool breeze, playing that game where you ask each other all the slightly-scary-but gotta-know questions when you're first getting to know each other: what was the name of your last ex? Why'd you break up? Have you ever had an STD?

There was one question on my mind that I badly wanted him to ask. It terrified me, but I also felt like it would set me free. As though reading my mind, he said it: *have you ever been pregnant?* I told him the simple truth, *Yes*. I curled into him and buried my face in his chest so I could keep the emotions playing across my face private. He apologized in the kindest way, letting me know that he was both sorry that I'd been through that, and that he had raised this heavy topic during such a light-hearted conversation. *I didn't assume you'd have been through that*, he said. Then, he followed up with something that blindsided me. He told me he'd been in the same situation with his last girlfriend. I looked up at his face in shock. My perspective changed in that moment, as though one part of my vision had always been hidden and then suddenly the blinders came off. *Of course, men go through this too.* How had it never occurred to me?

Obviously, the broker had been through this with me, and of course my friends mentioned their own partners in their abortion stories. But because women are so front and center in the story, the men who are on the other side of the equation easily fade to the back. Later that week, at an outdoor concert, I looked around the crowd with new eyes. If roughly one in four women here had been through an abortion, then roughly one in four men may have been through the experience with them. It gave me new appreciation for truly how many lives have been touched or shaped by abortion.

Back in the bedroom, my head was swimming, as if there was nothing to anchor my mind in that moment. Blake pulled me close to him, comforting me and bringing me back to the room and the moment. He rubbed my back and twirled my hair, lost in his own thoughts. I wondered how things had ended with his ex. If he had been able to comfort her during their period of grieving. Or even if he had needed comfort himself. I didn't tell him my story but said instead that I still badly wanted a baby one day. He didn't react, wasn't afraid of my honesty, but instead kissed the top of my head and remained silent. That afternoon, another of my firmly held beliefs—that all men are terrified of 35-year-old women who are ready to be mothers—shook loose, drifting like leaves on the calm surface of an endless sea.

AS FOR WHETHER BEING *PRO-CHOICE* automatically means being *anti-life*? In the Roe v. Wade decision, the justices writing the majority opinion said, "We need not resolve the difficult question of when life begins. When those trained in the respective disciplines of medicine, philosophy, and theology are unable to arrive at any consensus, the judiciary ... is not in a position to speculate as to the answer."

I have found peace with my belief about whether an abortion ends a life through deep and extensive personal reckoning. You've been on this journey with me, but I can only offer personal viewpoint on this from the place where I have landed, not as any kind of guiding counsel, as the justices were also reluctant to do in Roe v. Wade. Though there is still the occasional day where I question the choice I made, I simultaneously wish for a world where all women have agency over how our futures play out. Not only in terms of our reproductive freedom, but in every area of life. A vision that rapidly expands to depict a world in which everyone has a seat at the table. A world where solutions to societal problems take into account how each and every life will be impacted. And now, on the heels of what were slow but sure advances in women's equality, a "murder" charge that could carry a sentence of death. How is this *"pro-life"*?

In a similar form of backlash, following the election of the first African American president in the United States, it's not entirely surprising (though still horrifying) to me that we wound up with a white supremacist in the Oval Office. As painful as this is, if anything, it highlights how far we have come, and much farther there is to go. With the death of Ruth Bader Ginsberg and her replacement on the Supreme Court, Amy Coney Barrett, there is a great deal of speculation that Roe v. Wade may soon be overturned. Abortion (and women's rights generally) have become a less fashionable issue, what with the mountain of other, seemingly more pressing issues society faces today. However, we'd be remiss to overlook abortion and women's rights, as they are part and parcel of every conversation about equality—from #metoo to Black Lives Matter. There are rays of hope for women though, in the election of The Squad in 2018, the young women who stand at the forefront of The Climate Mobilization, and advances in some nations around the pay gap.

That said, it is increasingly clear that our present-day systems, from finance to healthcare to agriculture, are restrictive, divisive, and damaging to us as a society and the greater global ecosystem. Our planet is reaching a breaking point. If we want to avoid the mass unrest that an increasing number of social and climate scientists are predicting, we must make changes to archaic ideas and structures that are built on exploitation and inequality.

Again, perhaps because of my privilege, I believe the world we live in is generally more friendly than hostile—but the overall progress of humanity over time has also continued to prove this to be true. There are less deaths due to warfare and homicide with each passing year; we are making slow gains on lessening poverty globally; and young people like Greta Thunberg or those active in the Sunrise and Extinction Rebellion movements give me hope that we may yet see remarkable advances in how we address climate change. And history has also shown us that for every expansion there is a contraction.

Given the current backlash against abortion, I'm all the more thankful that I was able to make what I know was the right choice for me and my body when I decided to end my pregnancy. It makes me grateful to have come of age in the America that I did, grateful to be free, and grateful for all the sacrifices others have made along the way that made this possible for me. It makes me even more committed to marching forward in the direction of progress.

IN SOME WAYS, THE SHIFT towards feeling more gratitude for my own life following my abortion, prepared me for the uncertainty and fear we are living with against the backdrop of COVID. In my own way, I practice my brother's advice for hard times: *take it one day at a time and keep praying.* I watch the sunrise over the mountains. I break for an afternoon nap or to read a few pages of a good book. I love a cup of coffee and a Sunday drive. Today, I recognize what a miracle it is that I woke up with breath in my lungs. *I am fortunate to be alive. I have been gifted this precious human existence.* Focusing on these small daily gifts is not the same as turning a blind eye to the loss and tragedy happening outside my window. Quite the opposite. There have been cases at the care facility where my father lives, and in his condition he is extremely vulnerable. I have friends who have lost loved ones, and I live with the fear of him passing without me being able to say goodbye myself. But my gratitude acts as a ballast that keeps me on an even keel as we precariously surf this tsunami of change.

In the same way I face my fears around COVID, I am choosing not to look away from my abortion, and instead to be grateful for it all—bad and good. I am grateful for the life I continue to build because I had the freedom to make a choice. I recognize the preciousness of the life that never came to be, and try to honor that by living my life in a way that does not take one moment for granted. I have never been more aware of time. Each minute slips past, and we never know what's around the next corner. We can choose to see this as a curse, and live in fear, clinging to what we hold today, or as a reason to rejoice in what we have been given with each new breath we take.

Even four years ago, I don't know if I could have pictured a worse fate than the trifecta of having an abortion, being stuck in a bad relationship, and finding out my boyfriend had been cheating on me all along. In my eyes, there was no greater shame. Looking back, I can see how reaching this rock bottom gave me the *gift* of desperation. At that time in my life I would have done anything and everything in my power to change my circumstances. And I did.

Today, I live in a place of my choosing that suits my lifestyle. I do work that I find gratifying and am surrounded by friends who both support me and seek my support, bringing accountability to our relationships as we reach for our individual goals. Above all, going through what I can see now was an emotionally abusive relationship has taught me how to stand firm in my decisions, and always respect and defend my boundaries. I have reached this place of wholeness and integrity as a result of my own actions and my iron will. The beginning of all of this was the abortion. It was, at once, the hardest decision I have ever made in my life and the decision that set me free. I left a bad relationship, recognized and changed my limiting beliefs, and retrained my brain out of my knee-jerk reaction to try to solve all the world's problems here and now. Had I not been able to make that choice for myself, I wonder if I ever would have woken up to all the other choices available to me now.

COVID is a reminder that life itself is precious. In times of comfort and ease we can forget that mortality is our silent copilot each step of the way. Like my swim that fateful day, this is yet another wakeup call to examine how we choose to live, and not only remember what is important, but bring our focus to it. The toughest situations give us the broadest perspective on life. We remember the people we love, the life all around us, and the planet we call home. *I am fortunate to be alive. I have a precious human life.* In *The Book of Joy*—which tells the story of two religious heavyweights, the Dalai Lama and Archbishop Desmond Tutu, coming together for a week in 2015 to discuss what it means to live a joyful life—the Dalai Lama instructs us to remember those words every day when we wake up. Being so close to loss—being reminded of the fragility of our own lives and of those of the lives around us—reminds us of our impermanence and fixes our attention in the present, allowing us to look at life with gratitude and wonder.

nine

I met my new boyfriend, the swimmer, out beyond the break in the Pacific Ocean. The skies were stormy and gray towards the horizon, but clear overhead and with only a light breeze. The water was brisk, but not cold, and there was no swell that day—perfect conditions for swimming. I was out with a group that met up weekly in the evenings. Towards the end of our warmup, a friend and I were bobbing in the water near the buoys, waiting to get started on our "main set." My not-yet-boyfriend swam over and our mutual friend introduced us. We chatted very briefly about open water swimming (the joy, the fear), before he jetted off for one last solo warmup lap on the buoy line. He had swum in college, so his strokes were powerful and even. His shoulder and upper arm muscles rippled beneath olive skin as he swam away, energetic and seemingly unafraid of striking out alone.

After a half hour or so of swimming, our group was out of the water, rinsed and in dry clothing. We hung out to watch the sun go down, enjoying the mellow vibes that seem inherent to a California beach at sunset. A group of older men were playing reggae nearby, the sound drifting easily on the breeze. Empanadas and beers had been passed around our group, and the sky was turning ever deeper shades of pink, purple and blue. I stood mostly near my girlfriends, but I couldn't help overhearing the swimmer making some very corny jokes, followed by an unmistakably hearty and infectious laugh. The memory is locked safely away like an old cassette in a drawer of keepsakes, waiting to bring a secret smile to my lips anytime I play it back.

Our connection started slowly. We saw each other out with friends, went for a couple of bike rides and runs together, and eventually I asked him out for Thai food one rainy evening. I had been in California for the better part of a year by then, which put me at about a year and change from when I'd had the abortion. Once we began to hang out daily, it was clear that a relationship was on the horizon, should we want to take the plunge.

The idea of a serious new relationship electrified me and terrified me in equal measure. I was in a good place and I knew it. All the hours spent journaling, questioning what I wanted my life to look like, and working with professional healers and helpers had honed my intuition. I had no doubts that this was the kind of guy I'd be crazy to pass up a relationship with. But I was afraid. Opening yourself up to love is scary! Heart pounding, *jumping off tall objects into deep water* scary. I talked to my girlfriends about him endlessly, and even took him on some double dates to meet them. But I was afraid to take the next step. Although time had passed, the feelings of betrayal and heartbreak from my last relationship were still fresh in my memory.

YEARS AFTER I FIRST READ The *Book of Joy*, and just after what would have been the due date of my pregnancy, I found myself recommending the book to a lot of people. It had been a while since I picked it up, and when I began reading it again myself, I immediately knew why it had risen up in my consciousness at that time: it contained exactly the message I needed to hear.

Perhaps because I was so near my due date, I was experiencing a lot of regret. For the first time since we'd split up, I also had the urge to call the broker. I had a recurring dream around that time in which we would meet to talk. I'd walk into a coffee shop or restaurant and we'd sit down across from one another, but from the first moment he'd open his mouth, I'd know: he's lying to me. I'd run out with him calling behind me, repeating all the same things he'd said to me when we were together: *Don't go. I love you. You're crazy.* Only in my dream, I did go; I'd run outside and get in this beat-up little sedan where I'd have to face ever more difficult obstacles to escape him, while he chased me in a large, shiny, brand new truck. The dream was never exactly the same, but always had the same elements—and I always got away.

I spent so much time trying to puzzle out the meaning of these dreams (aside from the obvious: *don't call him, he's a liar*). I realized that my conflicted emotions about the abortion had come back as I was approaching this milestone, and I wondered: had these feelings become habitual, like brushing my teeth before bed or drinking a glass of water right when I get up? Our society glorifies struggle and hopelessness (you need go no further than *any* news site—left or right—for evidence of this). We're also told over and over that *it's okay not to be okay*—a slogan that's intended as a comfort, but which many of us seem to take as life advice.

When I began to question if I should feel guilty about my abortion, I felt *guilt for not feeling guilty,* as if carrying this heavy emotion would be a suitable penance for what I'd done. I wanted out of that trap, but had a hard time reasoning with myself that I should feel anything other than lousy after what I had done. Then one day, I read a passage in *The Book of Joy* where the Dalai Lama says, "So many people struggle with being kind to themselves. This is really sad. You see, if you don't have genuine love and kindness toward yourself, how can you extend these to others?" This quote became my reminder that it's not only okay *to be okay,* but that I would be doing others a disservice by remaining stuck in those negative thought loops. When I was in a bad headspace I could be distracted at work, less likely to go see friends, and generally more of a burden and less of a help to the people around me. I'd rather be my best self to my friends and coworkers (and the world at large), and that requires me to be my best self to my *own* self first and foremost.

But even after realizing that we both *can* and *should* change our self-destructive habits, I discovered that they still tend to stick around. In the twisted depths of our suffering, it's almost like we don't want to feel better. As though the longer we hold on to what hurts, the longer we won't have to accept our losses or our hardships. Around the time I would have been due, I realized I was holding on to all of those emotions as a way to remain connected to the child I didn't have. As if in some way, if I couldn't keep that pregnancy, I could at least cling to my emotions about my loss, and my recurring nightmares instead.

Most days, I can pull myself out of boggy feelings and negative self-talk. But there are still times when I write in my journal how much I hate that I had an abortion. I hate that this is my "thing." The realization of what I've done hits me all over again, and causes me to pace around my living room, the very thought of it causing too much irritation for me to sit still. There are times when it feels like these thoughts will never stop dogging me. I've always wanted to write a book, but I never, ever, wanted to write a book about *this*. A big part of me still rebels against it. I have days when I decide I will not publish what I write, that this will be a memoir for myself. Or I promise myself that I'll stop writing, and just tuck this whole experience away in some dusty, overlooked corner of my soul, never to be spoken of again—a textbook example of repression. But then I stop. I remind myself I have a choice in how I perceive this experience. I observe my thoughts just like I did that day in the open water, noticing my level of panic, reminding myself: *I can do hard things.*

Instead of dwelling on what I cannot change—that this has become my thing—I choose to allow my abortion to be a part of me, and I also choose to love it. Not because this somehow makes it more okay, but because I choose to love all of myself, including the experiences I wish I had not been through. I will not exile this part of me, and I will not exile this part of any other woman who has made this choice for herself and her future, either. Instead, I will keep engaging this practice of self-acceptance. And then, one day, months after my due date had passed, I realized that I hadn't had any desire to call the broker, and that my recurring dreams had dissipated, along with the urge to keep picking at my wound.

THE IDEA TO WRITE THIS book came to me when I was hiking alone in the mountains near my new home. It was early summer, and we'd had a lot of spring rain, making the hillsides green and lush. The cloud cover was thick that day and I remember feeling like I was walking around Jurassic Park, just waiting for T-Rex to pop his head out of the bushes. I was in the *really good* phase where my life was so full of gratitude and joy that I began wondering, *what if?* I didn't have a framework for all of my thoughts, so they were jumbled and scattered and I felt pushed and pulled by them. Writing in my journal had always helped me move from a place of confusion to order, and I wondered if writing something longer-form would help me understand this thing I had been through in a more thorough, dynamic way.

As the idea became more fully formed over several days, I realized how far this would push me and how scary it would be to publish. The idea of my life, my emotions, my shame being laid bare for all to see was enough to nauseate me. But I also knew deep down, call it a woman's intuition, that this project was happening. It took me months to arrive at a place where I was ready, but I have never felt so called to something in my life. Day in and day out, the writing of this book has brought me fulfillment, purpose, connection. It has been cathartic to dig through the filing cabinets of my mind and reorder things in a way that makes more sense to me.

Writing it has also been the backdrop to my deepening connection with the swimmer. I had the idea for it around the same time that we met, but it was months into us being together before I told him about my abortion. We were in bed, talking quietly in the dark, neither of us quite ready to drift off to sleep. I had been working on the manuscript for this book for months by then, and not only did I know I needed to tell him, but I wanted to. I wanted for him to know me, inside and out, good and bad. The same way I showed him the scars on my knees from years of mountain biking, I felt ready to show him the scars on my emotional body. The things I don't think about every day per se, but every so often look down and am reminded: *this is a part of me.*

I was nervous to tell him, though there was never any doubt in my mind that he would accept this part of my story. I stumbled towards the topic for several minutes, which only gave my heart rate the time it needed to double in pace. I was leaning over him while he laid on his back, and I was surprised he couldn't feel my heart beating like a woodpecker against my ribcage. I finally said the words, *I had an abortion a couple of years ago,* tears dripping on his chest. He pulled me closer and gently kissed my forehead and expressed his sympathy for what I had been through. He told me he could not imagine what that was like, but likened it to a friend who'd been through a divorce, acknowledging that maybe it was an act of self-love. He couldn't have been more compassionate. Then he made a joke about the roof having sprung a leak, because something was dripping on his chest. I smiled. His corny jokes are the best.

A few days later we were both in the bathroom, getting ready to head to work. In between showers, teeth brushings, and other morning routine staples, the subject of starting a family came up, as naturally as a discussion about what to have for dinner: when it might make sense for us, and what it could be like to make the decision to do that. The swimmer is very logical, so he talked about all the ducks we would need to have in a row before we got there, and how exciting it would be the day we decided to stop using birth control. My mind drifted more towards the emotional. The act of making a baby, lying in bed together afterward, wondering, *is this the time it happened?* I imagined taking a test—together this time (not wishing I could get my two minutes back)—and the feeling of joy and gravitas when we found out that yes, we were going to be parents.

145

BUT THAT IS ALL IN the future, and for now I am content with my life exactly as it is. More than two years since my abortion, a feeling of peaceful joy—what I've also heard called spiritual radiance, or, my personal favorite, *enchanted contentment*—permeates my life. Every morning, I wake up before the sun and watch blue skies and palm trees take form outside my window as day breaks. Some days I have to pinch myself to remember that this is my real life. I have a small group of tight-knit friends that lift me up even more with their own good vibes, and I am still close with my family. My father's illness is progressing, rapidly at this point, and though this is unbearable to me, I try to always remember his zest for life. Today, I live walking distance to my work, and am surrounded by coworkers who care deeply about the world and who show it with their actions; I've never seen a company owner so committed to the wellbeing of their employees, or our community. I find beauty and peace and joy in the simple details of my life.

A recent Saturday found me running with a girlfriend, along a succulent covered hillside, past some bluffs, and wrapping up along the beach. The tide was rising, filling our running shoes with salty water. We had coffee afterwards and talked about life. When I got home, I read a book in the afternoon sun that pours in the bay window of my living room. I spoke to my mom and brother on the phone, and made a dinner of fresh vegetables and soba noodles with the swimmer. It was a completely unremarkable and utterly fulfilling day.

Joy is so often thought of as a "high" emotion, all giggles and laughter and excitement. But joy runs deeper than that. It is an emotion based in peace and contentment, as it must be in order to be sustainable. We're so often taught that joy is naive, that it doesn't have depth. But like all emotions, joy cannot exist without its counterpart, suffering. Seen this way, the strength of our joy is equal to the depth of our suffering. Something else I learned from *The Book of Joy*. Mine is a well-thumbed copy, creased and marked from traveling everywhere with me. The pages are yellowed, and the corners are no longer sharp, but instead slightly soft from being packed and unpacked, shelved and re-shelved. And of course, it has that old book smell. I love flipping the pages right in front of my face to inhale the aroma of ink and aged paper that hints at hours of pleasurable escape. On the dust cover, His Holiness and the Archbishop are pictured in profile, facing one another, grinning with glee. Just the image of the two bespectacled octogenarians laughing at one another is enough to bring a smile to my face. Early in the book the author notes, "Their joy is clearly not easy or superficial, but one burnished by the fire of adversity, oppression, and struggle."

The lives of these two great leaders are marked with stories of exile, inequality and the torture of their respective people. They explain that it's actually our experiences of fear, anger, grief, despair, loneliness, and suffering that awaken us to the opportunity to choose how we want to react to the experiences in our lives. If we are able to remain open-minded, we can see that problems which feel like the greatest obstacles to joy are actually just part of our paths. Having an abortion, and dealing with the ocean of thoughts and feelings that came with it, became part of my curriculum for life. As I processed each of the emotional waves that came in its wake, and realized that each of them had a positive counterpoint, I was finally able to weave joy more firmly into my soul.

The *Book of Joy* is, quite simply, my favorite book. I read it long before my abortion, and more than the spiritual or scientific explanations of joy, I was touched by the heartfelt and fraternal relationship between the Dalai Lama and Desmond Tutu. In their conversations, they consistently poke goodhearted fun at one another, and are often moved to tears recalling the stories of their lives. The book was healing for me to read, and touched on so many themes I value—compassion first among them. It was a guidebook when I needed it most, and, over time, learning from the ideas it held shaped the life I live today.

BEYOND IT BEING PART OF my personal journey, telling my story in these pages has also given me a personal perspective on the issues of abortion and women's rights. Dissecting how these issues fit into our society and world as a whole has given me a macro view of the importance, and interconnectedness, of equality, storytelling, and the hope for a better future. Let me explain what I mean.

Globally, we face a myriad of deeply complex issues, of which—at the time of writing—the coronavirus is currently taking center stage. There will be an "other side" to the pandemic, and on it we will continue to face a vastly more existential threat: climate change and a global loss of biodiversity. Watching the US government fumble their way through the pandemic response is terrifying. If we can't find humane solutions for this tangible, highly visible problem, how will we find a path through something infinitely more complex that operates on a similar, exponential scale? Well, we can start with the question of equality.

It is a documented trend that countries with female leaders are faring better with the pandemic. Perhaps because, as *New York Times* reporter Amanda Taub argues, "Having a female leader is one signal that people of diverse backgrounds—and thus, hopefully, diverse perspectives on how to combat crises—are able to win seats at that table." Once those seats are filled with people who come from different walks of life, leaders have the opportunity to hear every angle of a problem that needs to be addressed, and can move forward without blindspots. This means that not only will a leader hear from an array of scientists and economists, but they will also hear about communities that have been impacted in varying ways. Similarly, the Women's Liberation Movement in the 1960s recognized the importance of helping the Civil Rights Movement. They knew that an increase in equality for any one oppressed group is an increase in equality for us all. We will do well to remember those lessons today.

So what does this have to do with abortion, and the threat to women's reproductive rights posed by the arguments of the "pro-life" camp? Leaders of Black Lives Matter, as well as Extinction Rebellion and Sunrise, have studied successful non-violent campaigns—from the abolition of the caste system in India, to the successful dismantling of the apartheid government in South Africa. One thing these movements have all understood is the importance of art and storytelling. And, as Meera Shah explains in *You're the Only One I've Told*, "The movement toward abortion access is founded on stories ... they can help reduce stigma and normalize abortion experiences. However, sometimes the stories with the greatest potential to have an impact on people's thinking are hidden or kept secret. Many fear that sharing their story will invite shame, disappointment, and sometimes abuse."

It is thanks to the dissemination of information and knowledge that humanity makes progress, whether in matters of health, wealth, inequality, and so many other standards. The people who come together and organize—be it in a movement like BLM, a company (charity or for-profit), or, yes, even in politics—are accelerating this progress. And I believe our world can continue to improve, but only when everyone has a seat at the table, and we remember the importance of the arts—among them, storytelling.

In today's clickbait world it isn't hard to find drama-filled stories of destruction and hate, often designed to drive us ever further apart. Life imitates art they say, and stories of a dystopian future are being played out all around us. But it is us who take these stories in, believe them, and in turn become them. What's needed now are stories that act as a counterpoint: stories of love, change, redemption, acceptance, and peace. Stories that make us believe in human nature as inherently good, that show us what equality looks like, and how we can work towards a healthy planet.

And this story is my contribution. It feels like so long ago that I was standing in a hot, airless parking lot, debating with the broker whether or not we would be parents together. I was hurt and raw and felt barely able to care for myself. I had hit rock bottom and saw what had happened to me as a curse: the abortion would be my burden to bear, forever. But over the course of writing this book, I have healed.

Sharing my story has allowed me to name and find a home for all my feelings. It has given me the space to step back and see that for each painful, heavy emotion, there is a corresponding level of peace and joy waiting to find its seat inside my being. I set off on the writing process with an idea: if sharing my story could in some way alleviate the suffering of even one person, it would be worth the effort. I didn't know then that the person it would help most would be me.

about the author

Anna Wood is a writer and creator with interests spanning environmental activism, feminism, and technology. When she isn't working or volunteering, Anna can be found outside adventuring, or inside with a good book. She currently calls California, USA home.

acknowledgements

I am deeply grateful for the support of the many people who made writing this book possible. Ruby, you are at the top of that list. Thank you for lending me your courage when I couldn't find my own, for helping me find my voice, and for your overall guidance through this process. I am honored you selected me as an early client in your program, but feel even more blessed to call you my friend.

I'm grateful for the rest of the team that made this project happen: Thanks go out to Louise Androlia for the beautiful cover art- it is still a dream come true when I look at my book! Dr. Jennifer Mullan for the keen insights and kind handling of the most sensitive pieces of the manuscript. Bess for the careful edits and fine tuning. Chris for the many designs that brought all the disparate pieces together. Ashley Morey, thank you so much for reading my book! As soon as we started talking I knew this was meant to be. Thanks to LA Voiceover for the studio time, and John at Aloe Audio for the production of the audiobook. Finally, thanks to Jamie for getting the word out about this important work.

I thank my friends- Astrid, you believed in this book before I ever put pen to paper. I wouldn't have taken on the challenge if it weren't for your words of encouragement. Jenafer, you were the first person who read my manuscript and you couldn't have been more encouraging.

You have been so open with your journey in life and have been an inspiration and role model in how you've navigated what has come your way. Amber and Anna, you provided encouragement when the project scared me (and when the edits felt never ending!). Jenny, you are an inspiration and a pillar of strength. Thank you. Leanne, there are just no words. First of all, you'll always be my bestie. We have done so many miles and so much life together. I love you, friend. Thanks for being open with me from the beginning and being there for me through this whole journey.

I'm grateful that I was able to get help when I needed it, and I thank the kind professionals who were there for me: Noah my pshcyotherapist, Andria and Jennifer, two acupuncturists and healers of top caliber, and Liora. But most of all, Liora. Thank you for everything.

Thanks go out to my family, who have stood by me through all the ups and downs on this road called life. I don't know where I'd be without you guys. Mom and Dad, you continue to teach me and you both have the biggest hearts of anyone I know- thank you for passing on all that love (and sensitivity!). I am grateful to my brothers for always having my back, and for trying to show me an easier way in life. N, there is no one on the planet who knows me the way you do, and there is no one else on this planet I'd pick to spend a lifetime alongside. You mean the world to me.

And finally, to the swimmer. Finding you was the ultimate needle in a haystack: one human in all of the Pacific Ocean. I must be the luckiest girl alive. You are a rock to which I can anchor, and most importantly you are always authentically, uniquely you. Thank you for keeping me laughing. I love you.

Made in the USA
Middletown, DE
27 February 2021